A selection of

"BOIL IN THE BAG" MEDITATIONS

Ernest J. Hewitt

Each 'Menu' contains

A Reading
A Hymn
A Prayer
An Expressed Thought

MOORLEY'S Print & Publishing
23 PARK ROAD, ILKESTON, DERBYS., DE7 5DA · ENGLAND

Hymns and quotations under copyright and used by permission are
acknowledged throughout the book. Extensive Efforts have been made to
contact all known copyright holders; any unintentional infringement is
regretted and we ask the indulgence of any copyright holder affected

Scripture Quotations
Scriptures quoted/adapted from the Good News Bible published by The
Bible Societies/ HarperCollins Publishers Ltd., UK © American Bible
Society, 1966, 1971, 1976, 1992, used with permission.

ISBN 0 86071 391 1

"BOIL IN THE BAG" MEDITATIONS

This book is dedicated to the memory
of my mother who passed away
on Christmas Day 1985

The love you showed, the joy I knew
In sharing life and home with you
Are treasured memories still.

It was in the days following her death that, as I looked back over our fifty-seven years together, I realised what a great part she had played in my service to the community.

For forty of those years I had been a schoolmaster, Methodist Local Preacher and active member of The Boys' Brigade.

In each of these spheres of work I had appreciated the opportunity of 'getting my point across' by using illustrations, and for me, as for Him whose example I try to follow, the best illustrations are from real life - so I look back over my experience of working with young people and recall various incidents -

With some I supply the moral.
With others, you can supply the moral
As for the rest, they are just told,
        since a young child once said,
        "I like my teacher, she has no morals."

Ernest J Hewitt

AN INTRODUCTION TO

"BOIL IN THE BAG" MEDITATIONS

If you are looking for ideas - ideas to share with others as you prepare to take an Assembly or lead an Act of Worship - if you are looking for ideas for your own time of private devotion, this book has been designed and written with you in mind.

For over forty years I have had the privilege and the responsibility of speaking to young people in School Assemblies and Church Services as well as Bible Classes and Youth Club. It is a tremendous responsibility, especially if, like me, you not only have to speak to them but you also live among them for a large part of each week. Then the main quality these youngsters are looking for is sincerity, and the feeling that they are being addressed by someone who cares about them. I have kept this quality and approach very much in mind in the presentation and content.

"Boil in the Bag Meditations" is here to give you ideas - or, if you like, each 'menu' gives you 'food for thought'. I have attempted to present some fifty different outlines - taking you through the year from September to the summer holidays. Each theme has a 'menu'; suggestions for you to use (or reject) according to the circumstances. I am sure that as you read the various stories and my own personal illustrations and experiences, other illustrations of your own will readily come to mind and so my ideas can be adapted or expanded.

Finally let me say this, I have not just written these themes in order to prepare a book - but each one has been used - in some cases many times - and I have selected what I feel will give you a well balanced diet.

Menu	Title	Theme
	Autumn Term : (September - December)	
1	A lesson in mathematics	A new beginning
2	The Voice	An opportunity found
3	A question answered!	Who is my neighbour?
4	Karen of Berkeley, USA	Prejudice
5	Ghoti!	The sign of the fish
6	A strange bunch	Making the right choice
7	A lesson from East Enders	An opportunity lost
8	Nine out of ten	Harvest
9	The birthday present	Prayer
10	Opportunity Knocks	Peter the Fisherman
11	For Grandad	Remembrance Sunday
12	Trying to escape	Peace
13	His brother's brother	Jealousy
14	The Christmas Card	Advent 1
15	The second candle	Bible Sunday
16	The Christmas Number One	Advent 2
17	Short of the readies	Advent 3
18	There's a world outside	The Christmas Message
	Spring Term : (January - April)	
19	More mathematics	The year ahead
20	Instant conversion?	St Stephen
21	Clervaux Abbaye	Influence
22	Jim Peters	Determination
23	An election experience	Ambition
24	Inappropriate registers	Education Sunday
25	Sticks and stones	Names
26	Amazing Grace	John Newton
27	Library Duty	Cliff Richard
28	An English takeaway	Lent - Temptation
29	BBC Community Help	Lent - Apathy
30	Cashing in on the occasion	Mothering Sunday
31	Extracts from my diary	Lent - Conflict
32	F A Cup Winners	Palm Sunday
33	A strange greeting	Maundy Thursday
34	Wells cathedral	Good Friday *+ Suppl.
35	Concern for the individual	Easter Day
	Summer Term : (May - August)	
36	Footprints	The road to Emmaus
37	Simon Johnson	Forgiveness
38	Tens and units	Starting out to work
39	A Senior Citizen defined	Understanding
40	Confusion	Whitsun
41	On writing a book	The Trinity - 1
42	On giving instruction	The Trinity - 2
43	A schoolboy's dilemma	On being a critic - 1
44	Out of retirement	On being a critic - 2
45	Yours undoubtedly	Thomas
46	Taking second place	Barnabas
47	Through the keyhole	John Mark 1
48	Boys will be ... ?	The call of God
49	A second chance	John Mark 2
50	Without wax	Sincerity

Analysis of Bible Readings & Themes

Reading			Theme	Menu	H&P
Gen 4	v	2 - 9	Peace	S2	776
1 Sam 3	v	1 - 10	The Call of God	48	523
Ps 121	v	1 - 5	Ambition	23	421
Eccl 3	v	1 - 8	The year ahead	19	---
Isa 9	v	6 - 7	Advent 1	14	97
Isa 49	v	14 - 15	Mother's Day	30	367
Matt 4	v	1 - 11	Lent - Temptation	28	138
Matt 4	v	18 - 22	Peter the fisherman	10	141
Matt 7	v	1 - 5	On being a critic - 1	43	739
Matt 7	v	24 - 29	Out to work	38	746
Matt 9	v	9 - 11	Making the right choice	6	149
Matt 21	v	1 - 11	Palm Sunday	32	162
Matt 22	v	34 - 40	Understanding	39	802
Matt 25	v	14 - 30	A new beginning	1	790
Mark 14	v	42 - 47	Easter Meditation	S1	181
Luke 2	v	4 - 7	Advent	17	98
Luke 2	v	8 - 14	Christmas	18	110
Luke 4	v	14 - 22	Bible Sunday	15	88
Luke 5	v	1 - 11	The sign of the fish	5	804
Luke 9	v	1 - 10	Influence	21	315
Luke 9	v	57 - 62	Lost opportunities	7	798
Luke 10	v	10 - 37	Who is my neighbour ?	3	220
Luke 11	v	1 - 4	Prayer	9	525
Luke 17	v	11 - 17	Harvest	8	352
Luke 22	v	39 - 46	Conflict	31	---
Luke 22	v	54 - 62	Good Friday	34	180
Luke 24	v	13 - 32	The road to Emmaus	36	645
John 1	v	1 - 14	Advent 2	16	108
John 6	v	5 - 15	Jealousy	13	---
John 13	v	2 - 15	Maundy Thursday	33	145
John 14	v	15 - 26	The Trinity - 1	41	578
John 14	v	27 - 29	Peace	12	492
John 19	v	17 - 24	Apathy	29	178
John 20	v	1 - 16	Easter Day	35	190
John 20	v	24 - 29	Thomas	45	212
John 21	v	15 - 20	Forgiveness	37	521
Acts 2	v	1 - 8	Whitsun	40	312
Acts 2	v	22 - 24	The Trinity - 2	42	7
Acts 4	v	32 - 36	Barnabas	46	553
Acts 7	v	54 - 60	Stephen	20	699
Acts 11	v	22 - 26	Names	25	257
Acts 12	v	6 - 16	John Mark - 1	47	594
Acts 15	v	36 - 41	John Mark - 2	49	---
Rom 2	v	1 - 8	On being a critic - 2	44	748
1 Cor 2	v	1 - 9	Education Sunday	24	709
1 Cor 12	v	4 - 11	An opportunity found	2	295
1 Cor 13	v	1 - 13	Sincerity	50	742
Eph 2	v	4 - 10	John Newton	26	215
Eph 6	v	14 - 19	Cliff Richard	27	697
Col 3	v	8 - 11	Prejudice	4	806
Hebr 12	v	1 - 6	Determination	22	548
'For the fallen'			Remembrance	11	404

Analysis of Hymns with appropriate Readings

First line of hymn	H&P	Reading	Menu
Amazing grace (how sweet the sound)	215	Eph 2 v 4 - 10	26
An Upper Room did our Lord prepare	594	Acts 12 v 6 - 16	47
Christ be my leader by night as by day	709	1Cor 2 v 1 - 5	24
Christ is alive ! Let Christians sing:	190	John 20 v 1 - 16	35
Come and join our celebration	97	Isa 9 v 6 - 7	14
Cradled in a manger	98	Luke 2 v 4 - 7	17
Father lead me day by day	790	Matt 25 v 14 - 30	1
Give me joy in my heart (v2)	492	John 14 v 27 - 29	12
Give to me , Lord, a thankful heart	548	Hebr 12 v 1 - 6	22
God is love: his the care	220	Luke 10 v 10 - 37	3
God is our strength and refuge	-	Luke 22 v 39 - 46	31
God of mercy, God of grace	-	Acts 15 v 36 - 41	49
God's spirit is in my heart	315	Luke 19 v 1 - 10	21
Hark my soul ! It is the Lord	521	John 1 v 35 - 42	37
Holy, holy, holy, Lord God Almighty	7	Acts 2 v 22 - 24	42
How blest is life if lived for thee	421	Psa 121 v 1 - 5	23
How sweet the name of Jesus sounds	257	Acts 11 v 22 - 26	25
Hushed was the evening hymn	523	1Sam 3 v 1 - 10	48
It came upon a midnight clear	108	John 1 v 1 - 14	16
It is God who holds the nations ...	404	'For the fallen'	11
Jesu, Jesu, fill us with your love	145	John 13 v 2 - 15	33
Jesus call us o'er the tumult	141	Matt 4 v 18 - 22	10
Jesus put this song into our hearts	-	John 6 v 5 - 15	13
Just as I am, without one plea	697	Eph 6 v 14 - 19	27
Kum ba ya, my Lord, kum ba ya !	525	Luke 11 v 1 - 4	9
Lord Jesus in the days of old (v3)	645	Luke 24 v 13 - 32	36
Lord of creation, to you be all praise	699	Acts 7 v 54 - 60	20
Lord of the home, your only son	367	Isai 49 v 14 - 15	30
Lord speak to me that I may speak	553	Acts 4 v 32 - 36	46
Make me a channel of your peace	776	Gen 4 v 1 - 9	S3
May the mind of Christ my Saviour	739	Matt 7 v 1 - 5	43
O come all ye faithful	110	Luke 2 v 8 - 14	18
O Jesus Christ, grow thou in me	742	1Cor 13 v 1 - 13	50
O Loving Lord who art for ever seeking	798	Luke 9 v 57 - 62	7
O Master let me walk with thee	802	Matt 22 v 34 - 40	39
One more step along the world I go	746	Matt 7 v 24 - 29	38
One there is above all others	149	Matt 9 v 9 - 11	6
Our blest Redeemer, ere he breathed	312	Acts 2 v 1 - 8	40
Seek ye first the kingdom of God	138	Matt 4 v 1 - 11	28
Spirit of the living God.	295	1Cor 12 v 4 - 11	2
Teach me, O Lord, thy holy way	748	Rom 2 v 1 - 8	44
The church of Christ in evr'y age	804	Luke 5 v 1 - 11	5
The holly and the ivy	88	Luke 4 v 14 - 22	15
There is a green hill far away	178	John 19 v 17 - 24	29
Thine be the glory, risen conquering Son	212	John 20 v 24 - 29	45
This is the day, this is the day	578	John 14 v 15 - 26	41
To everything, turn, turn, turn	-	Eccl 3 v 1 - 8	19
Trotting, trotting through Jerusalem	162	Matt 21 v 1 - 11	32
We plough the fields and scatter	352	Luke 17 v 11 - 17	8
Were you there?	181	Mark 15 v 42 - 47	S1
What shall our greeting be	806	Col 3 v 8 - 11	4
When I survey the wondrous cross	180	Luke 22 v 54 - 62	34

A Word of Warning

If you are going to serve a 'boil in the bag' meal the last thing you would do is take the contents from the packet and place them, still in their frozen state, on the plate. In the same way, I hope you don't feel you can use this book by just taking one 'menu' at a time and reading it to the group for whom it is intended.

One of the first things I learnt, when training to be a teacher, was, that in order to teach Michael mathematics, it is important to know something about Michael as well as knowing about mathematics.

If you are using one of the 'menus' for a group you will obviously know something about the group - then get to know something about the various ingredients too and adapt them accordingly. With a 'boil in the bag' meal you have to find the right sized saucepan, and know for how long to immerse the different bags - in the same way with 'menus' some preparation is essential. No two people will attempt to get the same point across in exactly the same way.

Lastly, make sure you don't serve 'chicken supreme' to a vegetarian - with or without the rice.

THE FIRST COURSE

(Autumn Term)

"BOIL IN THE BAG" MEDITATIONS

Autumn Term : (September - December)

1	A lesson in mathematics	A new beginning
2	The Voice	An opportunity found
3	A question answered !	Who is my neighbour ?
4	Karen of Berkeley, USA	Prejudice
5	Ghoti!	The sign of the fish
6	A strange bunch	Making the right choice
7	A lesson from EastEnders	An opportunity lost
8	Nine out of ten	Harvest
9	The birthday present	Prayer
10	Opportunity Knocks	Peter the Fisherman
11	For Grandad	Remembrance Sunday
12	Trying to escape	Peace
13	His brother's brother	Jealousy
14	The Christmas Card	Advent 1
15	The second candle	Bible Sunday
16	The Christmas Number One	Advent 2
17	Short of the readies	Advent 3
18	There's a world outside	The Christmas Message

Menu Master 1

A new beginning

A lesson in mathematics

Reading - St Matthew 25 v 14 - 30

Once there was a man who was going on a long journey: he called together his servants and put them in charge of his property. He gave to each according to his ability, to one he gave five thousand silver coins, to another he gave two thousand, and to the other, one thousand. Then he left on his journey.

Hymns & Psalms 790

> Father lead me day by day
> Ever in thine own sweet way,
> Teach me to be pure and true,
> Show me what I ought to do.
>
> When my work seems hard and dry,
> May I press on cheerily
> Help me patiently to bear,
> Pain and hardship, toil and care.
> *John Page Hopps (1834 - 1911)*

Prayer: Think of all the things you did yesterday and remember the time that was wasted, the opportunities lost. Now think of the day ahead and all the things that have to be done and pray that we may use our time wisely and do the best we can in everything we undertake.

"BOIL IN THE BAG" MEDITATION 1

You may require a calculator to help you follow the accuracy of these calculations - they take a bit of believing.

Many youngsters at Secondary School have eight lessons a day and each lasts for 35 minutes - to make our calculations easier we will call that 36 minutes (since few teachers finish a lesson on time). That means that each week lessons last for a total of

$$36 \times 8 \times 5 \text{ minutes}$$
$$= 1440 \text{ minutes}$$

I know there are 52 weeks in a year, but allowing for the summer holidays (6 weeks), Christmas (2 weeks), Easter (2 weeks), Half Term holidays and the occasional day for teacher training and the like, to say a school year lasts for 40 weeks would be a very generous allowance.

This means that Secondary School pupils are at lessons for -
$$1440 \times 40 = \text{ minutes a year}$$
$$(\text{total } 57000)$$

That appears to give us a very large number until we start to change the minutes into hours and the hours into days.

$$\frac{57600}{60 \times 24}$$

Surprisingly this gives us a total of just 40 days!

That is about one-ninth of a year - you may like to compare that with the number of hours you spend watching 'the box'. An average of just 3 hours each day, means you spend more time watching TV than you do in lessons - and as for the amount of time you spend in bed! - the mind begins to boggle.

When we begin to think of our friends we realise that some of them are better athletes or sportsmen than we are. Others have a greater capacity for learning and always seem to do better when it comes to tests and examinations, but does that mean they will make a greater success of life? Not necessarily so, having ability is one thing, using it to the best advantage is another. Just think back a moment to the story Jesus told - here were three men, each was given a sum of money to use or invest, two out of the three made a profit; the third one put it in a safe place but failed to use it wisely to good effect. Older versions of the Bible do not talk about silver coins but talents and, in this case, perhaps that is a better word. We do not all have the same opportunities. Some, as we have said, are brighter than others, some have greater physical ability; but what if bright ones don't work at their lessons? What if those with the greater physical ability don't bother to train, or keep themselves fit. Of one thing we can be certain, whatever other things we have or have not got in life - there is one way in which we all start equal - we all have twenty-four hours in a day and it is how we use that time that really matters.

Menu Master 2

An opportunity found

The Voice

Reading - 1 Corinthians 12 v 4 - 11

There are different kinds of spiritual gifts, but the same Spirit gives them. There are different ways of serving, but the same Lord is served. There are different abilities to perform service, but the same God gives ability to everyone for their particular service. To one person he gives the ability to speak in strange tongues, and to another the ability to explain what is said. But it is one and the same Spirit who does all this; as he wishes, he gives a different gift to each person.

Hymns & Psalms 295

> Spirit of the living God,
>   Fall afresh on me.
> Spirit of the living God,
>   Fall afresh on me.
> Break me, melt me,
>   Mould me, fill me.
> Spirit of the living God,
>   Fall afresh on me.
> *Daniel Iverson*

Prayer: You have given us many gifts, and the opportunities to use them: help us O Lord, to accept the challenges of life in the sure and certain knowledge that You will never ask us to do anything, unless You are also prepared to give us the help and guidance to see that job through.

Amen

"BOIL IN THE BAG" MEDITATION 2

In the early sixties I was a keen spectator at both The Royal Tournament at Earls Court and The London Boys' Brigade Display at The Royal Albert Hall. Realising one show was put on by adults, the other by boys the two shows had much in common, the one big difference was that at The Royal Tournament, they had a commentator who kept the audience well informed and welcomed them with a cheerful, "Good evening ladies and gentlemen ..." About this time I received an invitation to serve as a member of the London Display Committee - a committee that consisted of a number of notable men in BB circles, including Douglas Peason-Smith (the son of the Founder), how could I refuse such an invitation and perhaps I could suggest they introduced that missing ingredient. After I had served on the committee for a year I did venture to suggest that we too had a commentator. I soon realised I was a lone voice - for after all, as was soon pointed out to me, the London Display had functioned efficiently since 1901, people had programmes, they knew what was coming, what need was there for a commentator to tell them? The next year I tried again, with about as much success - but I was still convinced I was right - the rest were wrong.

Fortunately for me, the following year The London District appointed a new secretary, his name was Gerald Walker. After a brief conversation with Gerald I soon realised he was a man who was prepared to back me. I put my idea forward for a third time, it was now discussed at greater length - but I still had my opponents and they were not prepared to give way. Then completely out of the blue one of them said, "Mr. Chairman, I've changed my mind. I'll back the proposal!" Then after a dramatic pause - he turned to me and added, "If you are prepared to do it!" I am still convinced he only said what he did to throw me off balance, and silence me once and for all.

To make a suggestion is one thing, to see it through is something completely different, especially something of this magnitude - after all it was to be in The Royal Albert Hall and the audience in those days was five thousand people at each of three performances. Yet as the challenge was made I instinctively knew I must accept - and I did. That was in 1965 and when in 1987, over twenty years later the Display had to move away from its regular venue due to the rising cost of such a production in such a place, I was still saying, "Good evening ladies and gentlemen welcome ... "

In 1988 the London Display moved to the Wembley Conference Centre and I was commentator there as well. It was a strange experience in many ways, my announcements were not made from the stage but from a box next to "K stairs", and only those near to me realised who I was or where I was. As a part of my preparation I would visit a number of the items to get some ideas for my introduction and commentary - it was on such an occasion, that I was asked if I would like to say a few words - as I started to speak to the boys, one young lad, who had obviously been to the show in previous years, immediately responded with, "Blimey! It's the voice." - but that's all I was to many thousands for all those years - a voice - how wonderful to have been given such a gift - and the opportunity to use it.

Menu Master 3

Who is my neighbour?

A question answered!

Reading - St Luke 10 v 25 - 37

A teacher of the law tried to trap Jesus. "Teacher," he asked, "what must I do to inherit eternal life?" Jesus replied, "What do the scriptures say? How do you interpret them?" The man answered, "Love the lord your God with all your heart, with all your soul, with all your strength and with all your mind. And love your neighbour as yourself." "You are right," said Jesus. So the man had still to ask, "But who is my neighbour?"

Hymns & Psalms 220 (v2)

None can see God above:
Neighbours here we can love:
Thus may we Godward move,
Finding him in others,
Sisters all, and brothers

Sing aloud, loud, loud!
Sing aloud, loud, loud!
  God is good!
  God is truth!
God is beauty! Praise him!

Percy Dearmer (1867 - 1936)
© Oxford University Press, used by permission

Prayer: May we never miss the opportunity of sharing with others, caring for others - that we might share with the poor and care for the lonely: Sympathise with the sad and encourage the depressed. Wherever we see a need may we do all we can to help in a practical and acceptable way.
Amen

"BOIL IN THE BAG" MEDITATION 3

The headmaster of a large comprehensive wished to give greater variety to the upper school assembly, he therefore invited experienced members of staff to speak to the pupils on a rota basis. Unfortunately nobody was asked to work out a theme for the talks and each of those chosen was not present when the others spoke. With the result that each of the first four chosen used the same story - 'The Good Samaritan'. This means that, either it was the only story they knew or, as I prefer to think - it came high on their list of tales worth telling, since it tells how we should react to the needs of others. As a point of interest, four of the teachers might have told that story but only one of the four gospel writers did. The Good Samaritan is well known - perhaps too well known - and therefore when we hear it we don't bother to listen properly - but isn't it the kind of story we read every week in the local paper? How often have you read of someone being mugged - either for their purse or wallet, or what is just as common these days, a fashionable tracksuit or an expensive pair of trainers. The man in the story lost everything, they left him completely naked, and he was so badly beaten up, if he could have died. Yet the first couple of people to find him didn't bother to do a thing - and what's more they were both on their way to church (or the equivalent). It was left to a foreigner - a Samaritan, who felt no love towards the Jews - to do what he could, and he did plenty, even if it cost him.

So why did Jesus tell this story? A well educated man was trying to trick him into saying something that would cause trouble and judging by the way the conversation went, Jesus would have made a good politician - he answered a question with a question and left it to the questioner to work out the answer for himself.

Educated man -   What must I do to receive eternal life?

Jesus -	What do the scriptures tell you?
Ed. m -	Keep the commandments - love God and your neighbour
Jesus -	Well done, that's the right answer.
Ed. m -	But who is my neighbour? (that's a trick question)

Jesus tells the story of the good Samaritan finishing with that all important question.

Jesus -	Which of these three do you think was neighbour to the man who fell into the hands of robbers?
Ed. m -	The one who showed kindness.

Notice the questioner could not bring himself to use the word 'Samaritan'.

In 1965 Sydney Carter used this thought when he wrote the song:

> When I needed a neighbour were you there, where you there?*
> When I needed a neighbour were you there?
> And the creed and the colour and the name won't matter,
> Were you there?

He then links this story with something else Jesus said - words recorded in St Matthew's Gospel (ch 25). So the song goes on:

> I was hungry and thirsty, were you there, were you there?
> And the creed and the colour and the name won't matter,
> Were you there.
> Wherever you travel I'll be there, I'll be there
> And the creed and the colour and the name won't matter,
> I'll be there!

Menu Master 4

Prejudice

Karen of Berkeley, USA

Reading - Colossians 3 v 8 - 11

But now you must get rid of all those things: anger, passion, and hateful feelings. No insults or obscene talk must ever come from your lips. Do not lie to one another, for you have taken off the old self with its habits and put on the new self. This is the new being which God is constantly renewing in his own image, in order to bring you to a full knowledge of himself. As a result there is no longer any distinction between Gentiles and Jews, slaves and free men, but Christ is all, Christ is in all.

Hymns & Psalms 806

What shall our greeting be;
Sign of our unity?
 'Jesus is Lord!'
May we no more defend
Barriers he died to end;
Give me your hand my friend -
 One Church, one Lord!
F. Pratt Green (1903 -)
© *Copyright, Stainer & Bell Ltd., used by permission.*

A Prayer: O Lord, we are so easily hurt and offended when other people tell lies about us, or jump to the wrong conclusions, without finding the true facts first.

Help us, in our dealings with others, not to make the same mistakes. Help us to be generous in our thinking, forgiving in our nature, and sympathetic towards those whose views are different from ours.

So help us to follow your example.   Amen

"BOIL IN THE BAG" MEDITATION 4

The same year as Sydney Carter wrote his song 'When I needed a neighbour' another composer, Ted Blake, wrote a song with a similar theme. His song was called 'Different from us'.

I've lived in the East End down Whitechapel Way,
The last man to want any fuss,
But the Jews were there, I'm sad to say -
They were greasy and hooked-nosed and after our pay;
We don't hate them, you know, we just want them to go -
For they're all of them different, so different from us,
They're all of them different, yes, different from us.

I've lived down in Smethwick, in Old Marshall Street,
The last man to want any fuss,
But the blacks came in on their filthy feet,
And we whites had to shun them and turn on the heat;
We don't hate them, you know, we just want them to go -
For they're all of them different, so different from us,
They're all of them different, yes, different from us.

I've lived a good life, and if God's good to me
(The last man to want any fuss)
I shall go to heaven and there I shall see
My Saviour - there's only one thing worries me;
He's Jewish by race with a dark swarthy face,
And He's certainly different, so different from us,
He's certainly different, yes, different from us.

© Executives of E.C. Blake, used by kind permission.

It is amazing how many people, even those who profess to follow Christ, manage to be prejudiced, or jump to wrong conclusions.

Karen was just sixteen years old. She lived in Berkeley, USA, where she had recently seen the film 'A Gentleman's Agreement' which told the story of a man who pretended he was a Jew and the resulting treatment he received. In Karen's opinion the film was far fetched and could never happen in real life. She decided to test her theory. Her father had given her a charm-bracelet for her birthday and when her friends asked what the charms were, she told them they were Jewish. In fact Karen was a Christian but that simple statement made her friends jump to the wrong conclusion. Some made her feel she was not as welcome in their company as she had been, others turned their backs on her completely. Fewer invitations to parties and fewer opportunities to visit their homes. In six weeks she had found out all she wanted to know and then confided in her teacher. As a result of their conversation an invitation was extended to the whole school to attend a 'B.A.R.P. Meeting' - no explanation was given as to what those letters meant. Many were curious and turned up just to find out. Karen was the speaker and she told them the initials stood for Berkeley Attacks Racial Prejudice. She told them of her six weeks as a 'Jewess', she told them how she now realised that prejudice was far more than just a word in a dictionary, it is something that warps and twists people's minds and attitudes. She now understood how it resulted in concentration camps in Germany and violence against the negroes. Her friends had learnt a lesson and so had Karen.

Menu Master 5

The sign of the fish

'Ghoti'

Reading - St Luke 5 v 1 - 11

When he finished speaking Jesus said to Simon, "Push the boat out further into the deep water, and let down for your nets for a catch." "Master," Simon answered, "we worked all night long and caught nothing. But if you say so, I will let down the nets." Later that day Jesus said, "Follow me, and I will make you fishers of men."

Hymns & Psalms - 804

Then let the servant Church arise,
  A caring Church that longs to be,
A partner in Christ's sacrifice,
  And clothed in Christ's humanity.

We have no mission but to serve
  In full obedience to our Lord.
To care for all without reserve,
  And spread his liberating word.
F. Pratt Green (1903 -)
© *Copyright, Stainer & Bell Ltd., used by permission.*

Prayer:
Help us O Lord, in our lives, to be symbols of your love, may we so care for others that they may see in us a sign that points them to you.
  We ask this prayer in the name of Jesus Christ, God's Son, our Saviour.
Amen

I don't have to look back at my old school reports to realise that spelling was always one of my weaknesses - how pleased I am that these days the word processor has a built in 'spell-check'. English must be a very difficult language to learn if it is not your mother tongue, that is why I am always very impressed by the fluency of most of those who visit us from the Continent. There was an occasion when a German teacher asked if I could tell him about the word 'ghoti' - and I had to admit it was a word I had never met. He then proceeded to give me the following explanation:

> Let us first consider the letter in the middle, it is an 'o' this letter is also found in the word 'women' and must therefore be pronounced like an 'i' as in 'ink'. Next we will look at the last two letters 'ti', these are found in a lot of other words, such as 'nation', 'station' or even in 'explanation' - these must therefore be pronounced the same as the letters 'sh' as in 'sheep'. This only leaves the first two letters, namely the 'gh' I find these in 'cough' and 'rough' and they are pronounced 'f'. We can not put the whole word together - so that 'gh' 'o' 'ti' becomes 'f' 'i' 'sh'
>
> Have you never heard of the word 'fish' - my friend asked - not even with your very popular English chips?

This made me think of three other ways of presenting the same word in three different 'languages' - perhaps you can recognise them! How about this one?

Did you recognise it as semaphore?
The second one is a little more difficult?

```
      . .         .         .        .
         .     .       .         . .
               .
```

That was Braille.
The third language is Greek, they spell it like this -

$$I \quad X \quad \theta \quad Y \quad \Sigma$$

It is made up of the five letters iota, chi, theta, upsilon and sigma - these are the initial letters of the Greek words for - Jesus - Christ - God's - Son - Saviour.

When you stop to think about it, it is a very suitable word since several of the first disciples were fishermen and Jesus once said, "Follow me, and I will make you fishers of men." He was asking these men to help him in the work he was doing, he wanted them to learn from him and then pass on that message in a practical way, by the kind of lives they lived. So that the qualities we see in the life of Jesus - kindness, concern, caring - could be seen in their lives too. The fish became a symbol in the early church so that Christians could easily recognise one another, nowadays it is often worn as a brooch or a badge - it shows the wearer is a Christians - one who cares, and is concerned about others.

Menu Master 6

Making the right choice

A strange bunch

Reading - St Matthew 9 v 9 - 11

As Jesus was walking along, He saw a tax collector, named Matthew, sitting in his office. He said to him, "Follow me." Matthew got up and followed him. While Jesus was having a meal in Matthew's house, many tax collectors and other outcasts came and joined Jesus and His disciples at the table.

Hymns & Psalms - 149

One there is above all others,
  Well deserves the name of friend;
His is love beyond a brother's,
  Costly, free, and knows no end;
They who once his kindness prove
Find it everlasting love.
              John Newton (1725 - 1870)

Prayer: Thinking of an iceberg; we see the bit that sticks up out of the water, but there are seven eighths lurking underneath where we cannot see it. People are like icebergs. There's a great deal more to every person than we expect by looking on the surface. Help us, Lord, to accept people as we find them. Some of your friends had some funny habits, but you accepted them for what they were and made them into new men and women - your disciples. Help us to remember your words, 'Judge not, that you be not judged'.
              Amen

"BOIL IN THE BAG" MEDITATION 6

I wonder how many parents have said to their children, "I don't want you playing with him." They may have a very good reason for making such a request, but why did the child make such a choice in the first place? There must have been something that attracted them to their new friend. Do you think Mary and Joseph might have had the same problem with Jesus, when he was a boy? Or did he change his ideas when he got older - I doubt it. Jesus' ideas about God were pretty well fixed by the time he was twelve, he referred to God as 'my Father' so I guess the same could be true about other relationships. For us, however, first impressions can often be deceptive, there's an old saying that goes something like this - "There's so much bad in the best of us, and so much good in the worst of us, that it ill becomes any of us to criticise the rest of us."

When we look at some of the people Jesus chose to be his followers, they were a strange bunch. Look at that story about Matthew, for example, here was a tax collector, a man who worked for the Romans, and to make matters worse realising most people did not understand the method of taxation (times haven't changed much) he was probably dishonest too; and yet when we read his Gospel, he says Jesus not only asked him to be a disciple but, he then celebrated the occasion by having a party, and what's more, he invited what seemed to be a lot of unsavoury characters to join him. In his story Matthew refers to them as 'other outcasts' - that suggests he was an outcast himself - but Jesus chose him regardless of that, and what's more, Jesus was quite happy to join them at the party.

Then there was Zacchaeus - a strange name for another member of that strange bunch - he was a tax collector too, and he was so unpopular that when he joined the crowd, in order to catch a glimpse of Jesus, they pushed him away and he was forced to climb a tree, but Jesus spotted him and then invited himself to Zacchaeus' house for a chat. Now consider Andrew, Peter, James and John, they were all fishermen, so I wonder what their language was like at times? You could hardly imagine them as 'gentle, meek and mild'. In addition to this we know that Peter could be very impetuous - act first, then think about it afterwards, and that happened with him on more than one occasion - even after he had become a disciple. But later events have shown Jesus made a wise choice in choosing each of these men. Somehow he could see and appreciate that part of their personality and character that seemed to be hidden from others.

Making the right choice is not always easy. Have you ever been faced with having to choose who will be the captain of a team - or who will hold a position that gives them a certain amount of responsibility? How do we make such decisions, how do we judge what kind of people others are, and how do we decide who will make the best friends or a partner in life? We never really get to know the whole person - the real person - we only get to see a part, or in some cases we only see the part we want to see. A colleague of mine, and strangely enough, his name was Peter, once compared people to icebergs - you only see the bit that sticks out of the water - and that is only one eighth of the whole thing.

Menu Master 7

Lost opportunities

A lesson from 'EastEnders'

Reading - St Luke 9 v 57 - 62

Jesus said to another man, "Follow me." But that man said, "Sir, let me first go back and bury my father." Jesus answered, "Let the dead bury their own dead. You go and proclaim the Kingdom of God". Another man said, "I will follow you sir, but first let me say good-bye to my family." Jesus replied, "Anyone who starts to plough and keeps looking back is of no use to the Kingdom of God."

Hymns & Psalms 798

O Loving Lord, who art for ever seeking
  Those of thy mind, intent to do thy will.
Strong in thy strength, thy power and grace bespeaking,
Faithful to thee, through good report and ill-
William Vaughan Jenkins (1868-1920)

Prayer: O Lord, so often when we are watching television or reading a book, we look at the attitude of other people and become so critical of their attitude and actions and yet we are just as guilty of the faults we find in them. How did you put it Lord? "Why look for a speck of dust in your brother's eye when you have a plank of wood sticking out from your own?" May we see ourselves as we really are, and with your help, be more honest with ourselves and more considerate of others. Amen

"BOIL IN THE BAG" MEDITATION 7

Those who follow 'EastEnders' may well remember the episode in which Arthur Fowler came to a crisis in his life, mind you, I suppose that had happened many times, but the one that stands out in my mind was during January 1992. Arthur had always tried to be a family man caring for and supporting his wife, Pauline, and their son Mark and daughter, Michelle. Even when his daughter had an illegitimate child by the father of her best friend, Arthur stood by her. His son had always been a tearaway, leaving home when he was still in his 'teens' and for ages the family had no idea where he was, but when he returned he was accepted back and his father even attempted to get his son to work with him as a gardener in a small family business. Then came the bombshell. For some time they had believed that Mark was hiding something from them and they were right, he caught AIDS from the girl he had been living with when he left home. Up to this time he had only confided in a friend - he wanted to tell his parents, he needed their help and support so much, but how do you tell them a thing like that - then at Christmas time, he told them what the circumstances were - his mother came to terms with it, even if she didn't really understand what was happening - his father on the other hand made his son feel like an outcast - but as the story went on, one felt Arthur was not happy with the way he was treating his son, there was just nothing he could do about it. Eventually he broke down completely - he lied to his wife, telling her he had made it up with Mark - the breach had been healed - but she knew the truth. In a very emotional speech he said, "How many times have I said, if I had the chance of this, or if I had the chance of that I would grab it with both hands, if only I had had the opportunity - how many times have I said that? But I have had many of those chances, and many of those opportunities I wanted never really passed me by, I never had the courage to reach out and take them, I didn't want change, I didn't want to make waves, I didn't want to rock the boat. Then something like this happens, my son walks in and says, 'Dad, I've got ... this disease, it's probably going to kill me, so what do I do?' I have a go at him, I snip and snap - I don't think about him - I think, why did he have to tell me? He's making waves, he's rocking the boat!"

So many miss the chances that come their way, they are not prepared to put themselves out, not prepared to study or train. The Arthur Fowlers of this world - those who have had the opportunities - but they didn't have the courage to reach out and take them, or what is worse, they were just lazy. Their reaction is, 'leave me alone, don't rock the boat'. One of the saddest young men I ever saw was in Year 11, it was the end of the autumn term, certificates were being awarded for good progress or consistent effort. All his friends had qualified in one way or another, Richard hadn't, and the look on his face told its own story. He had missed his opportunity.

Now, how would you react to the challenge of Christ - when you feel you should try to live the kind of life he has told us about - being more honest with ourselves - more considerate to others? How would you react to that? Would your answer simply be, "Don't rock the boat, Lord, don't rock the boat."

Menu Master 8

Harvest

Nine out of Ten

Reading - St Luke 17 v 11 - 17

Jesus was going into a village when he was met by ten men suffering from a dreaded skin disease. They stood at a distance and shouted, "Jesus! Master! Take pity on us!" Jesus saw them and said to them, "Go and let the priests examine you." On the way they were made clean. One man - a Samaritan - saw that he was clean and came back praising God in a loud voice. Jesus said, "There were ten men who were healed, where are the other nine?"

Hymns & Psalms 352

We plough the fields and scatter the good seed on the land,
But it is fed and watered by God's almighty hand:
He sends the snow in winter, the warmth to swell the grain,
The breezes and the sunshine and soft refreshing rain.

All good gifts around us are sent from heaven above;
Then thank the Lord, O thank the Lord, for all his love.
M. Claudius (1740 -1815) tr. J.M. Campbell (1817 - 78)

Prayer:

God, whose farm is all creation,
    Take the gratitude we give:
Take the finest of our harvest,
    Crops we grow that we might live.

All our labour, all our watching,
    All our calendar of care,
In these crops of your creation,
    Take, O God: they are our prayer
John Arlott (Hymns & Psalms 344)
© *Copyright The Executors of John Arlott. Used by kind permission*

"BOIL IN THE BAG" MEDITATION 8

How many times have you heard small children corrected by their parents when, having been given a few sweets or small gift they have failed to say, "Thank you." Maybe you can recall when you were young, or even when you were not so young, someone having to prompt you with those familiar words, "Now, what do you say?" How embarrassing it can be! But we are all guilty of it at some time - even if we have not been corrected. Luke, who was a doctor, tells us of ten men who were healed but only one bothered to return and say 'thank you' to Jesus. I have a number of things that mean a great deal to me - not that they are valuable in themselves but they do have great sentimental value, and when I look at them they remind me of happy occasions or of the many friends I have known over the years. Three of these are tankards. One was presented to me by the Golden Age, a group of senior citizens for whom I organised a weekly club as a part of the community work within the school, another came from members of staff and pupils during my twenty-fifth Continental tour and the third to commemorate forty years of service in The Boys' Brigade. Each is suitably inscribed, each says 'Thank you'. How I appreciated those two words.

Every year towards the end of September or early in October you will see notices outside churches announcing the dates of the Harvest Festival Services. Many people who do not make a habit of going to church regularly do make a point of attending these special services. For one thing the building is made to look specially attractive, being decorated with bunches of flowers in addition to a fine display of fruit and vegetables. Very often the children form a procession, each child carrying a gift such as a loaf of bread, a piece of coal or a basket containing various kinds of food. These gifts together with those other things on display are often taken to the elderly, sick or needy after the services are finished. The whole thing is the way the congregation say 'Thank You' to God for the harvest he has provided. As the hymn puts it

"We plough he fields and scatter the good seed on the land
But it is feed and watered by God's almighty hand.
He sends the show in winter, the warmth to swell the grain
The breezes and the sunshine and soft refreshing rain."

An elderly gentleman was standing at the gate of his well-kept garden. A lady commented as she passed by, "It is wonderful what God can do with a piece of ground!" The old man thought for a minute and then he said, "I suppose it is, but you should have seen it when he had it on his own." Congregations meet to say 'Thank you' to God, and at the same time remember all those who have helped in any way to provide the daily essentials of life. That means not only farmers and fishermen but also those who transport the food or work in the factories where the food is processed and packed. It does not stop there either, for the food has to be stored, sold and finally prepared as a meal. When you stop to think about it, it is quite a team effort. We all rely on what others do for us - remember to say 'thank you' - and the best way to say thank you - is not just in words - but in actions. What is the point of saying thank you and then being a right little pain.

Menu Master 9

Prayer

The birthday present

Reading - St Luke 11 v 1 - 4

One day Jesus was praying in a certain place. When he had finished his disciples said to him, "Lord, teach us how to pray, just as John taught his disciples." Jesus said to them, "When you pray say:
Our Father in heaven, hallowed be your name.
May your kingdom come, and your will be done,
on earth as it is in heaven.
Give us today our daily bread,
and forgive us for the things we do wrong.
as we forgive everyone who does wrong to us."

Hymns & Psalms 525

Someone's praying, Lord, kum ba ya,
Someone's praying, Lord, kum ba ya,
Someone's praying, Lord, kum ba ya,
O Lord, kum ba ya.

Prayer: Lord, we have learnt how important it is to go to various people for help and advice, so teach us how to come to you in a similar way, to bring to you our problems and the things that concern us, and give us the right frame of mind to accept the answer we get - even if it means disappointment at the time.   Amen

"BOIL IN THE BAG" MEDITATION 9

In view of the fact both his parents were at work, Peter was looked after by a 'nanny', a kind of residential child-minder. He was well cared for but not spoilt, although on special occasions, he usually got the present he wanted. This was the case when Peter was coming up to his fifth birthday and when his parents asked what he would like, he chose a new bicycle. On the night before the big day, when it was time for bed, he was no trouble, the sooner he went to sleep, he thought, the sooner he would be awake and see his present for the first time. Having put on his pyjamas, and with his nanny in attendance, he knelt beside his bed and prayed the kind of prayer you would expect from a child of that age ....

> "Bless my mummy and daddy, and please make my dog Toby better, he hasn't been very well today. And please Lord, let the sun shine tomorrow - it's my birthday and I want to go for a ride on my new bicycle. Thank you, God. Amen."

As you can well imagine he was awake very early the next morning, and immediately rushed to the window - to his great disappointment it was pouring with rain - by this time his nanny was already in the room and watching him as he looked out of the window. Rather thoughtlessly she said, "It looks as though God did not hear your prayer, Peter!"

"Yes He did," came the swift reply, "but He said 'No'."

That young lad had learnt something many older folk have never learnt - saying your prayers is not a short cut to getting your own way. The disciples once asked Jesus to teach them how to pray - that doesn't mean they couldn't or didn't, for as Jews, they had no doubt said their prayers from an early age but Jesus' prayers were so different. They were real, a conversation with God, in the same way as we might speak with someone on the telephone, not the use of an answering machine where we sit back and wait for a positive reply to our requests. It is worth looking in depth at the prayer he taught his disciples - the prayer we all know only too well. Perhaps that is the trouble, we do know it too well and therefore when we say it, it becomes a meaningless string of phrases, and we do not stop to think about what they mean. Take the phrase, 'Your will be done' - not 'my will' - in other words if what we want is unacceptable, be prepared to take 'No!' for an answer.

It is also worth remembering Jesus said, "Don't go looking for long words or complex statements - that's what the Pharisees do, they believe the more they say, the more chance they have of being heard. Don't worry if your thoughts are simple ones, just be sincere in what you say." In his book 'The way I see it', Cliff Richard talks about his attitude to prayer. He has a set time each day which is given to some kind of devotion but there are many other times when he feels the need to pray as well. For example, he always prays before a stage performance - he doesn't get down on his knees or anything like that - but as he is putting on his make-up, he quietly commends what he is doing to God; or to use his own phrase, "I'm letting God in on the act".[1] When you stop and think about it, that's not a bad definition for prayer either, letting God in on the act, in other words, working together with God.

[1] Cliff Richard: The Way I see it. © 1968 used by kind permission of Hodder & Stoughton Ltd.

Menu Master 10

Peter the Fisherman

Opportunity Knocks

Reading - St Matthew 4 v 18 - 22

As Jesus walked along the shore of Lake Galilee, he saw two brothers who were fishermen, Simon (called Peter) and his brother Andrew, catching fish in the lake with a net. Jesus said to them, "Come with me, and I will teach you to catch men." At once they left their nets and went with him.

Hymns & Psalms 141

Jesus calls us! O'er the tumult
   Of our life's wild restless sea,
Day by day his sweet voice soundeth,
   Saying, 'Christian follow me.'

As of old apostles heard it
   By the Galilean lake,
Turned from home and toil and kindred,
   Leaving all for his dear sake.
                    Cecil Frances Alexander (1818 - 95)

Prayer: Lord Jesus, we thank you that the first disciples left everything to follow you. We thank you that in obedience they travelled far and wide, facing danger and hardship, to preach and teach in your name.

We thank you that we too can be your disciples - help us to be just as trusting and obedient   -   seizing the opportunities that present themselves.

"BOIL IN THE BAG MEDITATION" 10

A group of young radio operators were sitting together waiting to be interviewed for an important job - as they talked to one another the sound of tapping could be heard in an adjacent room - the potential interviewees continued talking with the exception of one young man who got up, opened the door of the room where the sound was coming from, and closed the door behind him. The tapping stopped - but their conversation continued. After a short while the young man appeared again and told them they could all go home. The tapping they had chosen to ignore was a message in morse code - the message said, "The first one into my office gets the job".

A lot of time is spent in preparing young people for 'job opportunities'. The writing of C.V's, interview techniques, careers lessons and conventions, all have an important part to play. There was no such preparation in the days of Jesus and even if there had been, no one could have foreseen the circumstances that presented themselves to Simon when he met Jesus at Lake Galilee. When he first started work Simon was just an ordinary young man doing an ordinary job, not an executive type or one who could become, in public life, a County Councillor or a Magistrate. He was a fisherman, working for his father.

The time came, however, when he changed his occupation and found himself in a managerial role. He didn't apply for the job, he didn't see it advertised in the local paper - it was just given to him. Given, that is, after he had taken the opportunity offered by a man he knew very little about. A man who had been a carpenter. What could a carpenter know about a fishermen? Probably very little, but he knew a great deal about people - by just by looking at them - and when he looked at Simon he saw a man with great potential. So much potential that he even gave him a nickname. "Your name might be Simon, son of John," Jesus said, "but I am going to call you Peter - because Peter means a rock, a firm foundation." Jesus could see in this person one on whom he could build a society, something that would last, and has lasted for nearly two thousand years.

Peter took the opportunity that presented itself to him; he was prepared to completely change his way of life, he was prepared to make the sacrifices such a change would bring - he found the job brought greater responsibilities than he had at first realised. Responsibility meant privilege and prestige but there came a time when he failed to match up to those responsibilities - in fact he completely 'lost his bottle' when Jesus was arrested, but then so did all the other disciples - even so, Peter later found the help and strength to overcome the unenviable position in which he had placed himself.

We do not all have the same opportunities, we do not all have the same gifts or qualifications - but do we use the opportunities that come our way. Do we develop the gifts and talents we have, and use them to best of our ability? How many times have you watched a football match when one team seems to spend most of the game in their opponents half - but they simply waste opportunity after opportunity - then the other team then get a breakaway and score the vital goal. They found an opportunity, and they used it!

Menu Master 11

Remembrance Sunday

'For Grandad'

Reading - 'For the fallen' - R L Binyon

> They shall not grow old as we that are left grow old;
> Age shall not weary them, nor the years condemn,
> At the going down of the sun and in the morning
> > We will remember them.
> > We will remember them.

Hymns & Psalms 404

> It is God who holds the nations in the hollow of his hand;
> It is God whose light is shining in the darkness of the land;
> It is God who builds his City on the Rock and not the sand;
> > May the living God be praised!
>
> When a thankful nation, looking back, has cause to celebrate
> Those who win our admiration by their service to the state;
> When self-giving is a measure of the greatness of the great;
> > May the living God be praised!
> > > *F. Pratt Green (1903 -)*
> > > © *Copyright, Stainer & Bell Ltd., used by permission.*

The Kohima Epitaph

> > When you go home
> > Tell them of us and say
> > For your tomorrow
> > We gave our today

"BOIL IN THE BAG" MEDITATION 11

Remembrance Day followed its familiar pattern. Ex-Servicemen's contingents, Pre Service Units and representatives from the various youth organisations had paraded from the Police Station in Grays. Following a service led by the Vicar, and the band of the Salvation Army accompanying the hymn singing, many wreaths had been laid at the War Memorial. As the parade moved off towards the Saluting Base a number of those watching started to move away as well. It was at that moment that the three year old son of the Commanding Officer left his mother's side and made his way to where the wreaths were, then, taking the poppy from his coat he gently placed it on the ground. His mother had followed wondering just what he intended to do, then seeing what he had done, asked him why. "It was for Grandad," came the short reply. The grandad he had never known, the grandad killed by war.

Every year services like that are held in villages, towns and cities all over the country. They are held on the nearest Sunday to November 11th since it was on the 11th hour of the 11th day of the 11th month that the Armistice was signed to end the First World War in 1918. Some people still call it Armistice Day, others, Poppy Day and if you want to know why poppies are used in this connection, the tradition goes back to the days of that same war when red poppies flowered where the fighting took place in Belgium. A Canadian Medical Officer, Colonel John McCrae, was inspired to write this simple verse: -

> In Flanders' fields the poppies blow
> Beneath the crosses, row on row
> That mark our place, and in the sky
> The larks, still bravely singing, fly
> Scarce heard amid the guns below.

In 1921 a new organisation was formed, The British Legion (the word Royal was added during its Silver Jubilee in 1971) and they used the poppy as a symbol of sacrifice. Millions of poppies and many thousands of wreaths and crosses are made in the Legion's own factory at Richmond which employs many disabled servicemen. Each year The Royal British Legion holds a Festival of Remembrance at The Royal Albert Hall in London. It is a very moving and spectacular occasion held in the presence of many members of the Royal Family and seen by millions of people on television. Perhaps one of the most moving moments is when, after the various units have given a fine display of musical and physical activities, they all return for a Service of Remembrance - during this service trumpeters play the Last Post and this is followed by two minutes of silence - during the silence poppies fall on those assembled in the arena - one poppy for each person killed as a result of enemy action. It is a time of great emotion when one realises the price that has been paid for the freedom we have. It is not just those killed in the two great wars, who are remembered, but also those who gave their lives in the Falklands, the Gulf War and, much nearer home, those killed as a result of terrorism in Northern Ireland and many places in England such as Deal, Knightsbridge and even the City of London itself.

'We will remember them.'

Menu Master 12

Peace

Trying to escape

Reading - St John 14 v 27 - 29

"Peace is what I leave with you, it is my own peace that I give you. I do not give it as the world does. Do not be worried or upset, do not be afraid. You heard me say, 'I am leaving, but I will come back to you'. I have told you this now before it happens, so that when it does happens, you will believe."

Hymns & Psalms 492 (v2)

Give me peace in my heart, keep me loving
Give me peace in my heart, I pray.
Give me peace in my heart, keep me loving
Keep me loving till the break of day
Sing hosanna! sing hosanna!
Sing hosanna to the King of Kings!
Sing hosanna! sing hosanna!
Sing hosanna to the King!

Prayer: O God, our Father, you are a God of peace, help us to have peace in our relationships with others. Give us understanding and a forgiving nature in our dealings with others. Keep us from being quick to take offence. Help us to control our tempers and our tongues. Help us to remember that other people have a right to their views and opinions just as we have. So help us to treat others as we wish them to treat us.
Amen

"BOIL IN THE BAG" MEDITATION 12

The Germans will greet you with, 'Guten Morgan', the French with, 'Bon jour' and, providing they don't simply say 'ullo, the British will greet you with, 'Good morning'. The Hebrew speaking people also have a greeting, for them it is 'Shalom'. It means neither good morning, nor good day. It simply means 'peace'. Like the other greetings it expresses a hope - it means far more than an absence of war it means 'may everything go well for you', with the understanding that the source of such well-being is God. 'Peace' is a word that means different things to different people. Many think of peace as a state of affairs to be maintained - in other words no more war - The Christian says it is a way of life to be created.

Whenever you listen to the news or read a newspaper, you become very much aware of some of the dreadful things that are happening in the world today. Political unrest, people constantly living under the threat of death because of their religion or belief not to mention the constant appeals we hear for food and clothing for those who live in those countries where famine and poverty seem to be almost the way of life. Even in our own country things are little better for many people, think of those who exist in a 'cardboard city', those who are constantly being harassed because their colour or culture is not acceptable.

To many, such stories have become so commonplace that they fail to realise the desperate situation others are in - some do realise and try to do something about it. One young man who was deeply concerned and tried to help improve things, felt his efforts were being totally ineffective. He came to the conclusion that the whole world was going rotten and the best thing he could do was to leave his home and join a group of Christians who were seeking a holy life. Consequently he entered a monastery - he became a Trappist Monk - a very strict order founded over three hundred years ago in France. Together with his fellow monks, he took vows of poverty, chastity and obedience, and the characteristic Trappist vow of silence. For the rest of his life he devoted his time to the common life of the Order and prayed for the evil world he had renounced. He now felt 'at peace'.

One of those who would have caused that young man anxiety and concern, was a fairly young girl - the eldest child of a large family. Her father had died and her mother had great difficulty in making ends meet. This meant that when her friends went out with others after school or at weekends, she was indoors looking after her brothers and sisters as well as doing a great deal of the housework. She had no time to call her own, she seemed to be at everyone's beck and call. Eventually she started work, in some ways the pattern changed very little but at least she made new friends including a young man, who was quite well off and offered her a new start in life. Here was an opportunity she must take. She turned her back on the family and went to America with her boy friend. In her own words, "I want time to enjoy myself, I want a bit of peace".

The dictionary says, 'peace is a freedom from disturbance, a feeling of friendship, a quietness of mind'. The hymn says 'to have peace in your heart, you must love and care for others'.

Menu Master 13

Jealousy

His brother's brother

Reading - St John 6 v 5 - 15

Jesus looked round and saw that a large crowd were coming to him, so he asked Philip, "Where can we but enough food to feed all these people?" Philip answered "For everyone to have even a little, it would take more than two hundred silver coins to buy enough bread." Another of his disciples, Andrew, who was Simon Peter's brother, said, "There is a boy here who has five loaves of barley bread and two small fish. But they will certainly not be enough for all these people."

Hymn: Jesus put this song into our hearts

Jesus taught us how to live in Harmony
Jesus taught us how to live in Harmony
Different faces, different races, he made us one,
Jesus taught us how to live in Harmony.

Jesus taught us how to be a family
Jesus taught us how to be a family
Loving one another with the love he gave
Jesus taught us how to be a family.
Graham Kendrick
Copyright © 1986 Thankyou Music, P.O. Box 75, Eastbourne,
East Sussex BN23 6NW - Used by permission

Prayer: Give me a listening ear, O God, that I may hear Your voice calling me to high endeavour. Too often have I been deaf to the appeals you have made to me, but now give me courage to answer, 'Here am I, send me.' And when any one of my human brothers, cries out in need, give me an open ear to hear in that cry Your call to serve You.

Amen

"BOIL IN THE BAG" MEDITATION 13

I've always felt sorry for Andrew - the one who was Simon Peter's brother. Different Gospel writers each give their own version of the various stories concerning Andrew but the one I prefer reading with regard to the 'call of the disciples' is the one in St John's Gospel - it must be basically true, since John himself was also involved in this incident. Jesus had spoken to two would-be followers and invited them to join him for the evening. The story then goes on:

> "One of them was Andrew, Simon Peter's brother. At once he found
> his brother Simon and told him he had found the Messiah. Then he
> took Simon to Jesus."

So there it is, Andrew was one of the first two to follow Jesus - I wonder who the other one was - I believe it was John himself. He never mentions himself in his own Gospel. Nevertheless one was Andrew who is mentioned thirteen times in the Gospels and on six of these occasions it refers to him as 'Simon Peter's brother'. Does this suggest that Peter is more important, and yet it was Andrew who introduced Peter to Jesus in the first place. It must be tough living in the shadow of your brother. One of the things I always tried to do, as a teacher, was to treat each pupil as an individual and not to constantly remind them of the achievements of someone else in the family.

Regardless of this as the story develops, there is no jealousy, no bitterness; Andrew is prepared to accept things as they are. He simply accepts the position he is given although Peter has a far more prominent place. In fact on three very special occasions, namely

> the raising of Jairus' daughter (Mark 5),
> on the Mount of Transfiguration (Matthew 17)
> and in the Garden of Gethsemane (Matthew 26)

we read that three disciples were singled out to be with Jesus - each time it was, Peter, James and John.

Far too many people spoil themselves by wanting what someone else has, be it position or possessions - what they call 'keeping up with the Joneses' - such an attitude has ruined many a life. The trouble is they never want anything for themselves, until they see someone else with it.

Does this mean therefore that Andrew lacked ambition, some may put that interpretation on his story. I believe Andrew was an ambitious person, and he saw that ambition realised on more than one occasion. If we return to the story mentioned above, 'he introduced his brother to Jesus'.

Look at John, chapter 6, read the well known story of the loaves and the fishes - who found the lad and introduced him to Jesus? Andrew did. Now turn to chapter 12. Philip met some Greeks and wasn't sure what to do, he turned to Andrew for help - Andrew introduced them to Jesus, he introduced them a better way of life.

When you think about it, that is not a bad ambition to have. It is something positive and gives a great deal of satisfaction. Find a way to help others rather than being jealous of them.

Menu Master 14

Advent 1

The Christmas Card

Reading - Isaiah 9 v 6 - 7

> A child is born to us! A son is given to us!
>> And he will be our ruler.
>
> He will be called, "Wonderful Counsellor,"
>> "Mighty God," "Eternal Father,"
>> "Prince of Peace."
>
> His royal power will continue to grow: his kingdom will always be at peace. He will rule as King David's successor, basing his power on right and justice, from now until the end of time.
>> The Lord Almighty is determined to do all this.

Hymns & Psalms 97

> Come and join our celebration, it's a very special day;
>> Come and join our jubilation, there's a new King born today.
>
> 'God is with us', round the world the message bring,
>> He is with us, 'Welcome', all the bells on earth are pealing.
>
> *Valerie Collinson (1933 -)*
>
> *Copyright © 1972 High-Fye Music Ltd., 8-9 Frith St., London W1V 5TZ*
> *Used by permission. All rights reserved.*

Prayer: Help us to pass on the message of Christmas, not just by the sending of cards, or the giving of presents, but by showing love and understanding - let us give those gifts that come from the heart - actions and attitudes that show we care.

In the name of the One, born in Bethlehem. Amen

"BOIL IN THE BAG" MEDITATION 14

You may find it hard to believe, but there are times when teachers can get irritable and bad tempered, especially at the end of term. Such a time for me, was during the last week of the autumn term. It had been one of those days when nothing had gone right. Because of frequent interruptions nothing I had planned had been completed, and so, after school I settled down in my office to catch up on the various bits and pieces. Within minutes of starting there was yet another knock at the door. For a moment I completely forgot some very useful advice I had been given many years before - 'whenever your thoughts are interrupted by the ringing of the telephone, don't answer at once, just forget yourself for a moment, slowly count to three, and think who might need your help and attention before you answer'. Unfortunately I realised, all too late, this golden rule should also be applied to a knock at the door; for on this occasion I immediately reacted with, "Come in." But there was no response. "COME IN," I called again, but this time a little louder, still no response. Impatiently I went to the door and opened it - you can guess the kind of mood I was in as I said, "Yes, what do you want?" A small eleven year old boy was standing there, in his hand an envelope - rather grubby by now for he had carried it with him all day. He handed me the envelope, which contained a card, and he simply said, "Merry Christmas, sir!" I invited him in and apologised for my attitude ... I never knew if he really understood what I was trying to say ... but it taught me a lesson I have never forgotten.

Another Christmas Card I will always remember was one I bought in September 1985. It was for that special person, although when I bought it I had no idea who would receive it. A couple of months later my mother was taken into hospital and as I started to sort out my cards it became obvious who would get that 'special card' - the words reflected the attitude of the nursing staff of Ward 19 at Orsett hospital. The card contained a poem by Helen Steiner Rice, the poem was called - 'Heart Gifts'

The poem speaks about life's richest treasures not being the things that we can buy. Money cannot measure 'Heart Gifts' such as 'A cheerful smile, a friendly word or a sympathetic nod. The poet views such things as treasures from God's storehouse.

Thoughtfulness, kindness and love cannot be bought or sold but the giver finds rich reward in giving them away.

As the nurse read the card, the tears in her eyes told their own story, I had found a 'heart gift' too. This same sentiment is also to be found in the Carol 'In the bleak mid-winter', by Christina Rossetti, which finishes with the words

> What can I give Him, poor as I am?
> If I were a Shepherd, I would bring a lamb.
> If I were a Wise Man, I would do my part:
> Yet, what I can I give Him - give my heart.

Menu Master 15

Bible Sunday

The second candle

Reading - St Luke 4 14 - 22

Then Jesus went to Nazareth, where he had been brought up, and on the Sabbath he went as usual to the synagogue. He stood up to read the Scriptures and was handed the book of the prophet Isaiah. He unrolled the scroll and found the place where it was written, "The Spirit of the Lord is upon me, because he has chosen me to bring good news to the poor. He has sent me to proclaim liberty to the captives and recovery of sight to the blind: to set free the oppressed and announce the time has come when the Lord will save his people." As he handed back the scroll Jesus said, "This passage of scripture has come true today, as you heard it being read."

Hymns & Psalms - 88 (The holly and the ivy)

> v3   And two is for the prophets
> And for the light they bring.
> They are candles in the darkness,
> All alight for Christ the King.
> *Emily Chisholm (1910 -)*
> *© Copyright, Stainer & Bell Ltd., used by permission.*

Prayer: Lord, thank You for Your word. Give us humility to listen; wisdom to understand and obedience to attempt your word. Give us strength to obey your word, through Jesus Christ our Lord, who is the Word. Amen

"BOIL IN THE BAG" MEDITATION 15

Many people associate candles with Christmas - in fact many churches hold a special service of 'Carols by Candlelight' on the Sunday before Christmas Day. In addition to this you will often find during the period of Advent (the four Sundays before Christmas) a wreath of holly intertwined with ivy placed somewhere at the front of the church, and on the wreath there will be four red candles with a white one in the centre. On each of the four Advent Sundays a candle is lit and then the white one on Christmas Day. This tradition is often accompanied by the singing of the Carol 'The holly and the Ivy' - singing the first and second verses on the first Sunday of Advent, the first three verses on the second Sunday and so on - if you look at the words of this carol you will see how appropriate such a tradition is - with the whole six verses being sung on Christmas morning. It also fits in with one of the many titles given to Jesus - 'The Light of the World'.

The third verse, sung on the second Sunday of Advent, speaks of the prophets and their Old Testament messages - this Sunday is often referred to as Bible Sunday. In the gospel of St John, the writer refers to Jesus as 'The Word' - he says "The Word was made flesh and dwelt among us". (John 1 v 14). In other words Jesus was the message of God in human form, a visual illustration of how to live. It might therefore be appropriate, at this stage, to look at one of the stories Jesus himself told - maybe this is a story you associate with a Harvest Festival service rather than Advent because it is that well known story of the sower. It must have been a very familiar sight for Jesus, even in his boyhood days to see the farmers out on the fields scattering seeds by hand. Many of those seeds would not fall as he intended, on the ground prepared for them. Some would fall on the pathway, on the stony ground on either side of the pathway or among the thistles. It goes without saying that modern technology has changed all that - at least in our country but some of the third world countries still rely on such primitive methods. What a waste of effort! What happens to that wasted seed? It cannot take root - it is choked by weeds, it starts to grow but the roots cannot go down deep enough. The Bible Society has adopted the figure of a sower sowing seed by hand as its emblem.

One day Jesus found there were so many people wanting to hear him speak that he had to sit in a boat and push out a little way from the shore. It could be that as he looked at the people he could also see on the hills, in the background, a farmer at work sowing his seed, and realising how much of the farmer's effort would be wasted, he used the illustration to get his point across. When the story was finished his disciples asked why he had told such a story, Jesus told them that the seed represented the word of God. He explained how many that heard what he was saying took no notice and carried on in the same old way, others listened and started to change their ideas but then outside influences came into play and they reverted to their former standards. Fortunately there were also those who really understood and, as a result, their whole lives were changed.

What happens to the seed in your case?

Menu Master 16

Advent 2

The Christmas Number One

Reading - St John 1 v 1 - 14

Before the world was created, the Word already existed: he was with God, and he was the same as God. From the very beginning the Word was with God. Through him God made all things, not one thing in all creation was made without him. The Word was the source of life, and this life brought light to all mankind. The Light shines in the darkness, and the darkness has never put it out. The Word was in the world, and though God made the world through him, yet the world did not recognize him. The Word became a human being, and full of grace and truth, lived among us.

Hymns & Psalms 108 (v3)

Yet with the woes of sin and strife
  The world has suffered long:
Beneath the angel strain have rolled
  Two thousand years of wrong:
And man at war with man, hears not
  The love-song that they bring.
O hush the noise, ye men of strife,
  And hear the angels sing!
Edmund Hamilton Sears (1810-76) alt.

Prayer: Let us pray that the light of understanding will abide in every human heart, and that each man will see himself in another - and another in himself.

May this bond of love, which is the true spirit of Christmas, unite all men in faith and hope.

Let us plan and work together in harmony so that the blessing of peace shall come to every nation.

May the special meaning of Christmas continue to guide us in all our future ways.   Amen.

"BOIL IN THE BAG" MEDITATION 16

In December 1990 a popular tabloid newspaper printed their views on some of the tunes in the Top Ten at that time and gave a short list, with an appropriate comment and the odds, of what could be the Christmas Number One. The 'short list' read: -

a) (20-1) - Geordie Boy by Gazza - For the sake of music, let's hope
he doesn't make it.

b) (14-1) - New Kids on The Block - This one's for the children - a real
Christmas cracker

c) (3-1) - The Turtles with Turtle Rhapsody - Love 'em, or hate 'em they are
everywhere and you just can't ignore 'em.

d) (3-1) - Saviour's Day by Cliff Richard - You just can't keep him down.
This slushy song will be a hit with the wrinklies.

It must have been a hit with more than the wrinklies - it made the Number One slot on Christmas Day. There is a popular Irish comedian who has the catch phrase "It's the way I tell 'em" - maybe with Cliff it's the way he sings them - and I don't just mean his musical ability, but his sincerity in singing about the One who has come to mean so much to him - he never hides the fact that Jesus is his Saviour. We may well ask what makes a song a 'Number One' - especially at Christmas - is it the singer? - the tune? or the words? I would like to feel it is the latter but I was proved wrong some time ago. On one occasion I was speaking to a number of youngsters and I told them I was going to read the words of a well known song, a previous 'Number One', when they recognised it they were to put up their hands. Few did, until I reached the last three lines.

It's Christmas time - there's no need to be afraid -
At Christmas time we let in light and banish shade,
And in our world of plenty we can spread a smile of joy,
Throw your arms around the world at Christmas time.
But say a prayer - pray for the others - at Christmas time
It's hard - but when you're having fun -
There's a world outside your window -
it's a world of dread and fear,
Where the only water flowing is the bitter sting of tears.
And the Christmas bells that ring there -
Are the clanging chimes of doom,
Well tonight, thank God it's them, instead of you.
And there won't be snow in Africa this Christmas time,
The greatest gift they'll get this year - is life.
Where nothing ever grows - no rain or water flows -
Do they know it's Christmas time at all?
Here's to you - raise a glass for everyone.
Here's to the them beneath the burning sun!
Do they know it's Christmas Time at all?
Feed the world - feed the world - feed the world,
Let them know it's Christmas time again!

Words and Music BOB GELDOF and MIDGE URE © 1984 Chappell Music Ltd.,
London. Reproduced by permission of International Music Publishers Ltd.

The words, written by Bob Geldoff, were sung by a host of stars who gave the proceeds from the record to people of the third world? Do we remember the message, the singer, or the tune?

message, the singer, or the tune?

Menu Master 17

Advent 3

A bit short of the readies

Reading - St Luke 2 v 4 - 7

Joseph went from the town of Nazareth in Galilee to the town of Bethlehem in Judea, the birthplace of King David. Joseph went there because he was a descendant of David. He went to register with Mary and while they were in Bethlehem, the time came for her to have her baby. She wrapped him in strips of cloth and laid him in a manger - there was no room for them to stay in the inn.

Hymns & Psalms 98 (v4)

And to those who never listened
To the message of thy birth,
Who have winter but no Christmas
Bringing them thy peace on earth.
Send to these the joyful tidings
By all people, in each home,
Be there heard the Christmas anthem:
Praise to God, the Christ has come!
George Stringer Rowe (1830 - 1913)

Prayer: At this special time of year, help us to remember what we are really celebrating - that Jesus is the reason for this season of fun and festivities and help us, O God, to remember him, his birth, his life, his love and let us share this time of celebration with him.   Amen

"BOIL IN THE BAG MEDITATION" 17

For many years the School Christmas Carol Service had followed the same pattern - the same carols - the same lessons - only the voices and the readers were changed. Then, one year it was decided to completely change the format of the service with selected members of staff and pupils reading their own answers to questions based on the theme 'The Whys of Christmas?' The questions were carefully chosen, but all related to the well known story. Why were the shepherds the first to hear of his birth? Why did the wise men visit the infant child? Why was Mary in a stable when her baby was born? I was invited to answer that last question. 'Why a stable?'

There were several answers I could have given but the obvious one seemed the most likely. Because of the census, life in Bethlehem was busy and hectic - people had come from miles around and what accommodation there was, was quickly filled. Mind you I have often wondered if the story would have had a completely different ending if Joseph had been a rich man, but he wasn't. God had chosen an ordinary working class home into which his son was to be brought up. Joseph was in no position to bribe the landlord to let him have something better - or to use a modern day phrase - 'he was a bit short of the readies.'

Some time ago I organised a tour for the school band. We gave a series of concerts at various places near the Rhine. One of these was at the castle in St Goar, unfortunately our coach was too long to travel round the bend leading to the castle. I had to find a vehicle to transport some of the band equipment for a distance of about three quarters of a mile - when I saw an empty minibus I felt this was my lucky day - the driver stopped at my signal, but failed to understand what I wanted, which is not surprising since I did not speak his language. I tried to express myself in a different way - but still he just shrugged his shoulders. In a moment of inspiration I took out my wallet, waved a couple of notes and tried again - suddenly the driver understood exactly what I wanted.

Joseph was not in the same position - he was 'a bit short of the readies'. The Bible tells us that the prophets forecast the coming of Jesus - including where He was to be born. Today almost two thousand years later life has changed very little - we are still too busy and life is still so hectic - especially at Christmas time - so that there is little, or even no, room for Jesus in our celebrations. No room, although it is His birthday we are celebrating - we still leave Him outside. Still in the stable and not in the house.

<u>No Room</u>
No room in the Inn for the one who came
To know all earth's sorrow, grief and pain,
Showing to all from Heaven above
The greatness and depth of the Father's love.

No room in the Inn, so in stable bare
Born into poverty, this Son so fair,
Angels are singing, His birth to proclaim
"Glory to God, all praise to His Name".

For if in this life, our desire has been this
To amass goods and possesions, His love we may miss.
So bring to Him now, your talents and time
And dwell in His love, which makes life sublime.

Mary Parr, from "The Wonder of Christmas"
© Moorley's, Ilkeston, Derbyshire

Menu Master 18

Christmas

There's a world outside!

Reading - St Luke 2 v 8 - 14

There were some shepherds in that part of the country who were spending the night in the fields, taking care of their flocks. An angel of the Lord appeared to them, and the glory of the Lord shone over them. They were terribly afraid, but the angel said to them, "Don't be afraid! I am here with good news for you, which will bring great joy to all the people. This very day in David's town your Saviour was born - Christ the Lord!"

Hymns & Psalms - 110

O come, all ye faithful,
Joyful and triumphant,
O come ye, O come ye to Bethlehem;
Come and behold him,
Born the King of angels:
O come, let us adore him, Christ the Lord.
18th Century. -Tr Frederick Oakley (1802 -80)

Prayer: O God, who gave us both sight and insight, open our eyes to see what we are really like, and to see the world as it really is. May we also see the way of Jesus for each one of us. Help us to follow His Way, pointing to signs of hope and bringing hope to others through our own Christ-like action.   Amen.

"BOIL IN THE BAG" MEDITATION 18

It was Christmas Eve 1985 - although I had visited the hospital at Orsett earlier that evening they still contacted me at about half-past nine informing me they were concerned about the sudden deterioration in my mother's condition. Needless to say I returned at once. For over two hours I just sat beside the bed as my mother lay motionless and asleep. In order to keep her cool, for her temperature had risen, two electric fans had been placed on the lockers - as they slowly turned the breeze caught the various Christmas cards fixed to wall with 'blu-tack'. One of these, I remember, was a musical card and as it was forced open from time to time it quietly and almost reverently played 'Silent Night'.

Eventually the night nurse appeared (not for the first time) and suggested they would like to make my mother comfortable - they had left a cup of tea for me in the small waiting room at the end of the ward. Although my mother had been in the hospital for a number of weeks these sudden changes in her condition and circumstances left me very confused in my thinking. I appreciated the gesture of a cup of tea but hardly felt like drinking it, I just stood and looked out from that third floor window and gazed at the scene below.

I had often preached about the two sides of Christmas - but I had never experienced it in the way it appeared that night. On the one hand there were the bright lights of the pub - I could almost hear the people singing - and then, nearby the church - light streaming through the windows - and as midnight struck, I could almost hear them singing as well, ... 'Yea Lord, we greet Thee, born this happy morning'. Two different worlds, each celebrating Christmas in their own way - but at that moment I realised there were not two worlds but three - the third world - for me it was not 'a world outside the window' but one close at hand, it was still 'that world of dread and fear', for behind me was the world of pain and suffering, the world of loneliness, and those who never knew what the future might hold. With such thoughts in my mind I realised there is really only one way to worship the Infant Christ at Christmas and that is by being mindful of the needs of others - and then helping them, in some practical way.

> At Christmas, there are many gifts
>   that are purchased with silver and gold,
>   dazzling in their splendour and breathtaking to behold:
> But the one true gift of Christmas is a gift from God above,
>   assuring ev'ry mortal man of God's enduring love.
> For with this Christmas gift of love our spirit is redeemed
>   and man at last possesses the peace of which he dreamed.

On that day we might attend worship and sing:
>   Yea, Lord, we greet thee, born this happy morning:
>   O come, let us adore him, Christ the Lord

But let us remember, true adoration, true worship is found in meaningful service - Jesus said, 'inasmuch as you did it to one of the least of these, you did it to me.' If we possess this Christmas gift of love, let us share it with others.

THE SECOND COURSE

(Spring Term)

"BOIL IN THE BAG" MEDITATIONS

Spring Term : (January - April)

Menu Master 19

The year ahead

More Mathematics

Reading - Ecclesiastes 3 v 1 - 8

Everything that happens in this world happens at the time God chooses. He sets the time for birth and the time for death, the time for planting and the time for pulling up. He sets the time for sorrow and the time for joy, the time for mourning and the time for dancing.

A song adapted by Pete Seeger

To everything, turn, turn, turn,
There is a season, turn, turn, turn,
And a time for every purpose under heaven.
    A time to be born, a time to die:
    A time to plant, a time to reap,
    A time to kill, a time to heal:
    A time to laugh, a time to weep.
To everything ......
© Copyright Stainer & Bell, used by permission

Prayer:

Teach us anew each passing year (day)
More readily to heed and share,
The gladness of rejoicing hearts
The burdens of another's care.

Replace despair with lively hope,
Darkness dispel with dawning light,
And where the night of sorrow reigns
May we bring joy, the day-star bright. Amen
© Freda Head (H&P 357) used by kind permission.

"BOIL IN THE BAG" MEDITATION 19

It was in September 1992 that Richard realised he had been at work for a year - his boss had told him that after a year he would get an increase in his weekly wage - Richard was not backward in coming forward and when he met his boss the conversation went something like this

Richard Am I not due for a rise Sir? I have worked here for twelve months now.

Boss   Is that so? Since 1992 is a leap year, you must have worked for me for 366 days - 24 hours a day.

R   No not 24 hours day Sir! I only work eight.

B   But that is only one-third of a day - in other words you only work for one-third of a year - 122 days! And do you work on Saturdays and Sundays?

R   No Sir. I don't work at weekends.

B   But there are 52 Saturdays and 52 Sundays in a year - so that reduces your total of days worked by 104 - leaving 18! Then, what about holidays? What holidays did you have?

R   I had a week in the summer - and a week for Christmas and the New Year.

B   So that leaves just four days - Good Friday, Easter Monday, May Day and Spring Bank Holiday! Richard, you haven't been to work at all, how can you ask for a rise?

By now Richard was totally confused, are you confused as well?

The first time I ever travelled abroad was by the Channel Ferry from Dover to Ostend in 1955. During that journey I got into conversation with a retired gentleman from Texas - he had made his money from oil and was on a world tour. He had already visited a number of places in Great Britain and was now travelling to Brussels before going on to Paris. In the course of our conversation I asked if he could tell me at what time we were due to arrive at Ostend. His answer, I have never forgotten. "Time," he said, "what is time? On the journey to England, aboard a large ocean liner, I was resting on the sun deck when an announcement was made that lunch was being served. Without thinking I got up and started to make my way to the dining-room but then I realised I wasn't really hungry. I had only reacted because it was time to do so - for over forty years I had worked to a set pattern each day, a slave to my watch. Man had invented the watch to be his servant - now it had become his master - with this thought in mind, I immediately took my gold Hunter watch from my pocket and threw it over the side. From now on I would only do what had to be done when I felt like it. What time do we get to Ostend? When we arrive."

In some ways we often feel like that man, why go to bed when we are not tired - and why get up when we are? Why keep to a set pattern each day? It is all a part of the discipline of life. In some ways it is good to be independent, but if that independence also means that we become unreliable what use are we to anyone? The correct use of time is important, and so is being 'on time' - or punctuality. We create a bad impression if we arrive late - constant lateness shows a lack of interest - that is why it is recorded in the school register and shown on school reports. We expect buses to run on time, we expect TV programmes to start on time - why them and not us?

Menu Master 20

Stephen

Instant conversion!

Reading - Acts 7 v 54 - 60

As the members of the Council listened to Stephen, they became furious and ground their teeth at him in anger. With a loud cry they covered their ears with their hands. Then they all rushed at him at once, threw him out of the city, and stoned him. The witnesses left their cloaks in the care of a young man named Saul. They kept on stoning Stephen who cried out in a loud voice, "Lord! Do not remember this sin against them!" He said this and died. And Saul approved of this murder.

Hymns & Psalms 699 (v2)

Lord of all power, I give you my will,
In joyful obedience your tasks to fulfil.
Your bondage is freedom; your service is song;
And, held in your keeping, my weakness is strong.
© *Jack Winslow (1882-1974)*
Used by kind permission of the Executers

Prayer: O Lord, we don't always realise how much our lives are influenced by the lives of others - even the type of clothes we wear or the way we style our hair - the things we say and the way we say them. Just as we copy others, others copy us. Help us to do nothing that will later cause to regret the example we have set.

Amen

"BOIL IN THE BAG" MEDITATION 20

A very valuable racehorse developed a limp in its front right leg. The owner called a vet but could find nothing to account for this condition. To make absolutely sure the vet used an X-ray machine, but the result was the same. The owner was very distressed, he not only thought a great deal of the horse it was also worth a lot of money and he dare not race it unless it improved. They sought a second opinion - this only confirmed the first, there was no reason for the lameness. As time went on they tried different ointments and bandaging but still there was no change - although the limp got no worse, it got no better. One morning a young stable lad approached the owner, and asked if he could make a suggestion. The owner said he was willing to try anything - if it would help. "Well," said the stable lad, "why not change the groom? The groom is responsible for the exercise and feeding, the groom therefore spends a lot of time with the horse and consequently, the horse spends a great deal of time with the groom. That groom also walks with a very pronounced limp." The groom was changed and the horse got better.

One of the better known stories in the New Testament tells how Saul of Tarsus who was so against everything that the early Church stood for, he was prepared to imprison, or even have murdered, anyone who dared to suggest they were followers of Christ. Miraculously Saul, who was later known as Paul, then found his whole life was changed and he too became a Christian. The story, recorded in the Book of Acts, tells how he was coming near to the city of Damascus, when suddenly a light from the sky flashed round him and he heard a voice saying, 'Saul, why do you persecute me?' Whenever I have heard people tell this story they seem to put too much emphasis on the word 'suddenly', they suggest it was an instant conversion - just like coffee - no preparation required. Personally I do not think it happened like that, I believe there had been some kind of preparation - Saul had been influenced by those he was persecuting - especially Stephen, the first Christian martyr.

For some people there may be a moment in their life when there is a sudden realisation that they want something completely different, but I still ask the question, 'how much of that sudden awareness depends on what has gone before?'

A young lady who approached her minister after the evening service and told him she had decided she wanted to be a Christian. He was so thrilled and immediately asked which part of his sermon had prompted such a reaction. She had to tell him, in an apologetic way of course, that nothing he had said had prompted her decision, it was simply the attitude and example of one of the girls at work. I am one of those queer folk (and I use that word advisedly) who are able to tell you the exact date on which I decided to dedicate my life to Christ - in other words to become a Christian in deed as well as name - the date was Sunday 28th. October 1945 - but there was nothing instant about that decision. For most of my life I had been influenced by others, people I had come to respect and admire - people who had shown me by their example the best way to get the most out of life. I suppose that's why I eventually wrote this book.

Menu Master 21

Influence

Clervaux Abbaye

Reading - Luke 9 v 1 - 6

Jesus called the twelve disciples together and gave them power and authority to drive out demons and to cure diseases. Then he sent them out to preach the kingdom of God and heal the sick. The disciples left and travelled through all the villages, preaching the Good News.

Hymns & Psalms 315

Just as the father sent me,
So I'm sending you out to be
My witness throughout the world -
The whole of the world.
    He sent me to give the good news to the poor,
    Tell prisoners that they are prisoners no more,
    Tell blind people that they can see,
    And set the down-trodden free,
    And go tell everyone
    The news that the kingdom of God has come.
Alan T. Dale (1902-79)
© Oxford University Press. Used by Permission.

A Prayer of St Teresa:
Christ has no body now on earth but yours,
    No hands but yours, no feet but yours.
Yours are the eyes through which must look out Christ's
    compassion on the world.
Yours are the feet with which He is to go about doing good.
Yours are the hands with which He is to bless men now.

"BOIL IN THE BAG" MEDITATION 21

In the early seventies I organised a number of school trips to Ludwigshafen-am-Rhein. In those days, the journey took a long time, as there were few autobahns, and so we spent the night at Clervaux (Luxembourg). During our stay we walked to the Abbey high above the village, it was an interesting trip, made all the more worthwhile for most of the children since there was a shop in the Abbey where they could buy presents and souvenirs - for youngsters, no trip is worthwhile unless you can spend. The following year we made a similar trip and again stopped in Clervaux. The children asked if they could go back to the Abbey and most made a beeline for the shop. That didn't surprise me - but what did, was what some of the boys bought - three of the eldest, ones I had taught for several years, each bought identical rings to wear on the small finger of the right hand. I smiled when I saw their purchases, but it also made me stop and think, since the year before I too, had bought an identical ring and I too had worn it on the small finger of the right hand - in how many other ways were they copying me?

One day Francis of Assisi was approached by two young men who told him they had heard he was a very influential preacher and it was their wish to hear him in action. "That's a strange coincidence," he responded. "Today is market day, I am using the opportunity to go on a preaching mission to the nearby village, perhaps you would like to come with me?" The small party immediately set out and soon reached their destination.

Francis seemed to be very much at home as he spoke to the various villagers and farmers who had brought their produce to sell. He addressed most by name and judging by his inquires about their health and families he obviously knew them quite well and took more than an average interest in their circumstances. Francis spent so much time in conversation that those who had come to hear him preach were getting rather impatient, waiting for him to stop and address the crowd, but he never did, and eventually they found themselves walking back the way they had come. "We thought we were going to hear you preach?" they said, "and all you did was talk to individuals!" "That is how I preach," said Francis, "I let the people know how much I care about them." The two men went thoughtfully on their way.

As I look back over the years I realise how much I have been influenced by the example and opinions of others, and in turn I have influenced them. We all influence others at all stages of life - brothers influence brothers, fathers influence sons, friends influence friends and teachers influence pupils. If others respect us or enjoy our friendship they copy our actions or agree with our views - whether our actions or opinions are right or wrong. That gives each of us a tremendous responsibility. It gives us responsibility in two ways - to set a good example for others to follow - and the responsibility to think things out for ourselves and not blindly follow what others do. 'I am what I am, because you were what you were' - I once said this of a man who was a Local Preacher and one who had greatly influenced my life. I said it, not because of his preaching, but because of the way he had lived.

Menu Master 22

Determination

Jim Peters

Reading - Hebrews 12 v 1 - 6

As for us, we have this large crowd of witnesses round us. So then, let us rid ourselves of everything that gets in the way, and of the sin which holds on to us so tightly, and let us run with determination the race that lies before us. Let us keep our eyes fixed on Jesus, on whom our faith depends from beginning to end. He did not give up because of the cross! Think of what he went through. So do not let yourselves become discouraged and give up.

Hymns & Psalms 548

Give to me, Lord, a thankful heart
  And a discerning mind:
Give, as I play the Christian's part,
The strength to finish what I start
  And act on what I find.

When, in the rush of days, my will
  Is habit-bound and slow,
Help me to keep in vision still,
What love and power and peace can fill
  A life that trusts in you.
            Caryl Micklem (1925 -)
         © *Used by kind permission*

A Prayer:

Good morning God, another new day,
More things to do, more things to say,
Today's a new pathway I haven't yet trod,
But I know you'll be with me,
  Good morning God.

"BOIL IN THE BAG" MEDITATION 22

In Oxford on May 6th 1954 Roger Bannister completed the mile in 3 min 59.4 secs. The first time any athlete had completed the distance in less than 4 minutes. Later that year I joined the crowd at the White City Stadium in London hoping to see a repeat performance; we were disappointed but what we did see was something just as outstanding, a one hour endurance world record attempt by Jim Peters. The target was a distance in excess of 11½ miles. The world record was not broken but Jim Peters did break the British record and then it was announced he would carry on running in an attempt to beat the 12 mile world record - again he was unsuccessful but again he beat the British record, and then to the great delight of the crowd, he managed to find the energy to complete a lap of honour.

Some years later Jim Peters accepted my invitation to act as the Inspecting Officer at the 2nd Grays Company Display. As we talked together before the event I told him I wanted to make reference to that event but was not sure of the date - to my great surprise he told me he couldn't remember either - the only thing he could remember was that after he had completed a couple of laps he realised he was beginning to get a blister on his heel. When I reminded him that he went on running for another hour , he simply said, "I know, but think how many people were depending on me, I couldn't let them down, could I?"

In 1988 The London District Annual BB Display moved from the Royal Albert to the Wembley Conference Centre. There were many advantages in such a move, but could we recapture the atmosphere that had become so much a part of the display and would the efficiency of those working behind the scenes be as high in such a different situation? From a personal point of view, after twenty three years as the commentator at the Royal Albert Hall this new venue presented quite a challenge. It was at the end of the evening performance, as I was packing away my belongings, that a lady approached me and said, "Not the same here, is it? It will take a lot of getting used to, and I'm not really sure if I want to." With that, she walked away. If I am going to be honest, that person summed up my feelings exactly. It was a new experience, a different experience - and as I drove home that evening I, too, wasn't sure I wanted to repeat it.

I did repeat it however, and the next year I was back again - and so was that lady - and again she came up after the display had finished. Remembering her comments from the year before, she said, "I did wonder whether it was be worth coming again, but then I have often wondered whether it is worth taking the Anchor Boys on Friday evenings - they can be so naughty you know. But as I watched and saw those young men being presented with their Queen's Badges, the highest award they could gain, I realised that one of them was the first Boy to join our Anchor Boys, ten years ago. It was worth it after all." With that she went on her way and I realised how much The Boys' Brigade, and all other youth organisations like it, depend on the dedicated efforts of such ordinary people who are prepared keep on working for others - even when the going is tough and they feel like giving up - but somehow they never do.

Menu Master 23

Ambition

An election experience

Reading - Psalm 121

> I look to the mountains:
> > where will my help come from?
> My help will come from the Lord,
> > who made heaven and earth.
> He will not let you fall,
> > your protector is always awake.
> The Lord will protect you from all danger;
> > He will keep you safe.

Hymns & Psalms 421 (v3 & 4)

> All day to walk beneath thy smile,
> > Watching thine eye to guide me still;
> To rest at night beneath thy care,
> > Guarded by thee from every ill.
>
> To feel that though I journey on
> > By stony paths and rugged ways,
> Thy blessed feet have gone before,
> > And strength is given for weary days.
> > > *Anonymous*

Prayer: Thank you for the present, the time in which we live and for all the opportunities we have for growing up, finding our feet and enjoying ourselves.

Thank you for the future, we can give thanks before it comes because we know it will carry your blessing. Help us to use it wisely, approaching it with ambition and perseverance so that those who come after us, will benefit from all that we have done. Amen

During the 1992 Local Elections I served as Presiding Officer at a Polling Station in Tilbury. As the voters reach your table you must establish their identity, to one gentleman I put the same questions as I had to everyone else - like the others he stated his name and address as requested, but then completed his answers with, "Mr Hewitt, Sir." I realised this was a novel way of introducing himself and reminding me I had taught him at Lansdowne Road School nearly forty years before. I was pleased I could still recognise his face; but that is more than I can say of another ex-pupil I met on the same occasion, this one I had taught twenty five years earlier - and what is more I didn't remember the incident that immediately came to his mind - even after all that time - apparently, during my last week at his school - Torells - I had held a mathematics quiz, awarding small prizes for the best sets of answers - he quickly added that he had long forgotten the mathematics - but he remembered winning a bar of chocolate. It's strange the things we remember.

I often come into contact with those I taught years before - but not always in a Polling Station - although there is another I met in just that way - her name was Kaye. I had taught Kaye only twelve years before, and I was able to recognise her at once. In view of the fact she appeared at a time when we were not very busy we had a fairly long conversation - recalling various personalities and incidents. In the course of our conversation she reminded me of a poem I had once used in assembly - it started with the words, 'Somebody said that it couldn't be done,' this I did remember, for I had used the quotation in assembly on a number of occasions (but only once, I hope, with any given group). What surprised me was that she then went on to recite the whole poem and told me it had come from a red book, which I had allowed her to take home so that she could make a copy of the words. It's strange the things we remember.

> Somebody said that it couldn't be done,
> But she, with a chuckle, replied,
> "Maybe it couldn't," but she would be one
> Who wouldn't give in till she tried.
> So she buckled right in, with the trace of a grin
> On her face: if she worried, she hid it,
> And she started to sing, as she tackled the thing
> That couldn't be done ... and she did it.

Ambition - determination - perseverance - three qualities that go together and we don't get far in life without them. One of the stories I told in connection with this poem, was of a car - a very old car - being driven at the Kirkstone Pass, one of the steepest climbs in England. One of the occupants said to the driver, "We'll never get to the top in this old banger." The driver replied, "We'll get nowhere if we just sit here and talk about it." Slowly but surely they drove on and they made it - all the way to the top - it was then that the same occupant looked back and said, "That's funny, it doesn't look nearly as steep from up here as it did from down there, does it?" - and that's worth remembering too.

Menu Master 24

Education Sunday

Inappropriate registers

Reading - 1 Corinthians 2 v 1 - 5

When I came to you, my brothers, to preach God's secret truth, I did not use big words and great learning. For while I was with you, I made up my mind to forget everything except Jesus Christ and especially his death on the cross.

Hymns & Psalms 709

Christ be my leader by night as by day
Safe through the darkness, for he is the way.
  Gladly I follow, my future his care,
  Darkness is daylight when Jesus is there.

Christ be my teacher in age as in youth
Drifting or doubting, for he is the truth.
  Grant me to trust him; though shifting as sand,
  Doubt cannot daunt me; in Jesus I stand.
Timothy Dudley-Smith (1926 -)
© Copyright - used by kind permission

A Prayer (from Companion to the Lectionary - Volume 3)

As you gathered your disciples around you on the hill-side, you have been in our midst as we worshipped, and you have confronted us in your word.

For this, Lord Christ, we bless you.

Make us, your disciples, one in your Name, a living sacrifice to your heavenly Father, that with our neighbours we may learn from you his will: for with him and the Spirit you are one God in truth and for ever and ever.

Amen
© Copyright - Epworth Press; used by kind permission

"BOIL IN THE BAG" MEDITATION 24

Speaking to a group of children at Linford Methodist Church one Sunday, I glanced at the suggested notes for this particular day - Education Sunday - they suggested, starting by asking the question, "What have you learnt this week?" Strangely enough, that very week, as a supply teacher, I had learnt a lot. I had been asked to cover an English lesson for Year 8 students (13 year olds) - work sheets had been prepared on the topic - 'Inappropriate Registers'. That was straight forward enough, providing I knew what was meant by 'inappropriate registers'. To be honest, I didn't. Fortunately the notes on the work sheet were very clear and after a short period of preparation I was able to tackle the lesson in an interesting way, since it came at a time when I had been studying the music and story of 'My Fair Lady' - the musical in which Henry Higgins attempts to teach Eliza Doolittle to "speak proper', like a lady does".

What is an inappropriate register? The work sheet explained it as follows:
Aim - To understand that people use different types of language depending on the purpose and the audience. People use, and understand, language in many different ways. The type of language used is known as the register and depends on:

      the speaker: who it is that is speaking or writing.
      the purpose: what the language is being used for.
      the audience: who is the listener or reader.

Do we always consider those we are speaking to and adjust what we say accordingly? I well remember a geography teacher when I was at school, who just sat at his desk for the whole lesson and dictated notes for us to copy and learn. One of my friends then discovered an old exercise book belonging to his uncle - who had been at the same school, ten years earlier - the notes were word for word the same. Nothing had been altered. The lesson may have been the same but the pupils were different, and so probably, were their needs and understanding.

Jesus was a remarkable teacher - he knew so much about those to whom he was speaking - he knew their needs - is that not why so many came to hear him speak? They said, "He taught with authority and not like the Scribes." They could understand what he was trying to say - he got his message across - because he understood their needs and could approach them in a positive way, using simple examples with stories taken from everyday life. Look at the stories recorded in Luke 10 and 15, many of his hearers had lost something that was as precious to them, as that coin was to the widow. Many parents had experienced the frustration caused by a son who had not acted in the way they had expected - the parable of the prodigal son was something they could identify with. Muggings were as frequent then as they are today - ethnic minority groups as despised - that is why the story of the Good Samaritan really went home. It was a part of their experience. Jesus knew his audience, he spoke their language. A man once said, "Why use one syllable, when six will do?" Big words may impress but they do not help us to understand. Jesus used the simple language of his hearers. We are all teachers, others learn from us - not only by our words, but also our actions - do we get our message across using the appropriate register?

Menu Master 25

Names

Sticks and stones

Reading - Acts 11 v 22 - 25

Barnabas went to Tarsus to look for Saul. When he found him, he took him to Antioch, and for a whole year the two met with the people of the church and taught a large group. It was at Antioch that the believers were first called Christians.

Hymns & Psalms 257

How sweet the name of Jesus sounds
In a believers ear!
It soothes his sorrows, heals his wounds,
And drives away his fear.

Dear name - the rock on which I build,
My shield and hiding-place,
My never-failing treasury, filled
With boundless stores of grace!
John Newton (1725 - 1807)

Prayer: Lord Jesus you called your followers by various names
You called them disciples - which means learners
You called them apostles - which means ambassadors
Above all, you called them your friends, and showed
    your great love towards them - not only by your
    life, but also by your death on the Cross.
May we be worthy to be called your friends, making us
        loyal and true in all we do.   Amen

"BOIL IN THE BAG" MEDITATION 25

I wonder if you have a nickname? Most people have, and if you haven't, I bet you have plenty of nicknames for other people - specially the teachers at school. There is an old saying, 'sticks and stones may break my bones, but names will never hurt me'. Personally, I don't think that is really true. There are times when we can be very cruel and unkind with some of the nicknames we use, and they are deliberately aimed at being hurtful, and you don't need me to make a list of them for you. What we are called, whether it is a name or a nickname, is very important to us. Some prefer to be called by their full Christian name, other prefer an abbreviated form and we must be careful we use the correct form when we speak to someone. If a boy has been named William, do we call William or does he prefer to be called Bill, or Will, or Billy? I have also known boys that, as they have got older, have delighted in taking on the Christian name of their father. Mark was like that, for years he wanted to be known as Geoff - I also knew Geoff, his father, then one day he announced he had reverted to being called Mark again. When I asked why the sudden change I was told he had opened one of his father's letters by mistake. He never told me what the letter was about. As a teacher I always asked the class I was taking for the first time, to write their names as they would like me to use them to make sure I got it right.

I also remember watching a quiz programme in which the Quiz Master was questioning a lad of fourteen on the subject of mathematics - the lad was very bright and obviously came from a very good family - on being told the contestant's name was Richard, the Quiz Master immediately asked, "What do I call you, Dick?" The reply showed absolute disgust as he said, "I think my parents would be offended if you did."

For the most part we are proud of our names - but that is not always the case. When one young lad was spoken to by a member of staff, the teacher used his surname, - his immediate reaction was to say, "Please don't use that name, Sir, I would prefer to be called John." It wasn't that he disliked the formality but he had two brothers in the same school, both were always in trouble - he didn't wish to be known by the same name. Sad, but true.

Many names in popular use today, started off as nicknames and were meant to be offensive and were used in a derogatory way, but somehow they stuck, and with the passage of time, and the work associated with the people they were intended for, their meaning has completely changed. Names like Christian and Methodist, would come into this category, people who professed to follow Christ and those who were methodical in their worship. When we think of names associated with the church, the name of one of the disciples, Peter, was a nickname too, and you can read about that in a different 'Menu' in this book - the same applies to Barnabas, his name was Joseph. Their nicknames were very complimentary and were given to them because of their attitude to life and the potential they showed.

If you have a nickname what does it show about you?

Menu Master 26

John Newton

Amazing Grace

Reading - Ephesians 2 v 4 - 10

For it is by God's grace that you have been saved through faith. It is not the result of your own efforts, but God's gift, so that no one can boast about it. God has made us what we are, and in our union with Christ Jesus he has created us for a life of good deeds, which he has already prepared for us to do.

Hymns & Psalms 215

Amazing grace (how sweet the sound)
That saved a wretch like me!
I once was lost, but now am found,
Was blind, but now I see.

Through many dangers, toils and snares,
I have already come.
God's grace has brought me safe thus far,
And he will lead me home.
John Newton (1725 - 1807)

King Charles the First's Prayer:
O Lord, make thy way plain before me. Let thy glory be my end, thy Word my rule: and then thy will be done. Amen

The Blessing:
And may the Grace of the Lord Jesus Christ be with us all. Amen

"BOIL IN THE BAG" MEDITATION 26

In 1967 a song, sung by Judy Collins, went to the Number 1 spot in the charts - it may be hard to believe but that song had been written two hundred years before. The writer's name was John Newton. He was born in London, and as the son of a sea captain, he went to sea in his father's ship when he was only eleven years old. Like most youngsters of that age he was happy-go-lucky, taking nothing very seriously, with certainly no thought for religion. In later life he wrote of those early days and told how there were times when he did not take life seriously, "I began to pray, to read the scriptures and keep a sort of diary - but alas, this seeming goodness had no real foundation and I soon gave it all up and became worse than before - instead of prayer, I learned to curse and blaspheme. The struggles between sin and conscience were often repeated - but after each relapse I sank into even greater depths of wickedness."

When he was seventeen years old his father managed to get a job for him in Alicante, Spain. The job offered excellent prospects but, since he was unwilling to accept discipline, and also due to his general bad behaviour, within a year he found himself sacked and sent home. In those days it was the practice of the Royal Navy to get recruits by means of a 'press gang' - 'compulsorily-volunteered' if you like. John Newton found himself the victim of such a gang and was taken aboard a man-o-war called 'Harwich' where he had a rough time. His father still had a certain amount of influence and managed to get him promoted to the quarter deck as a midshipman. Here life was much easier and he could have made a good career - but he got in with the wrong company, was constantly disregarding orders and finished up by deserting. He was caught, thrown into prison for forty eight hours and then publicly stripped, flogged, and degraded to the lowest possible rank. Eventually he was transferred to another ship and sailed to Africa, where, we are told, 'he engaged himself to a slave purchaser'. Apparently, he had deserted again. Eventually he became the mate aboard a slave ship, and then the master, but strangely enough it was at this time that he began to take life seriously again and used his free time to improve his education. He read a book called, 'Of the Imitation of Christ' and as a result his whole life was transformed - he realised that in spite of everything, God still cared for him.

He had a very varied and colourful life and was only thirty when he gave up the sea and took a job in Liverpool. It was at this time that he started to study Greek and Hebrew and applied to the Archbishop of York for ordination into the church - his request was refused - but six years later he was offered the curacy of Olney in Buckinghamshire and was ordained by the Bishop of Lincoln. Whilst at Olney he struck up a friendship with William Cowper - they both had an interest in hymn writing which resulted in the publication of the Olney Collection. Many of those hymns are still sung today - but perhaps the one that is the most popular is the one Judy Collins sang. On the 13th April 1972 it found its way to the top of the charts again, remaining there for 25 weeks, this time it was played by the Pipes of the Royal Scots Dragoon Guards. On both occasions the words and music were of the hymn 'Amazing Grace'.

Menu Master 27

Cliff Richard

Library Duty

Reading - Ephesians 6 v 11, 14 - 19

Put on all the armour that God gives you, so stand ready with truth as a belt tight round your waist, with righteousness as your breastplate, and as your shoes the readiness to announce the Good News of peace. At all times carry faith as a shield, accept salvation as a helmet and the word of God as a sword which the Spirit gives you.

Hymns & Psalms 697

Just as I am, without one plea
But that thy blood was shed for me,
And that thou bidd'st me come to thee,
    O Lamb of God, I come.

Just as I am, thou wilt receive,
Wilt welcome, pardon, cleanse, relieve,
Because thy promise I believe
    O Lamb of God, I come.
                        Charlotte Ellott (1789 - 1871)

Prayer of Ignatius Loyola:
    Teach us, good Lord, to serve thee as thou deservest;
        To give and not to count the cost;
        To fight and not to head the wound;
        To toil and not to seek for rest;
        To labour, and to ask for no reward,
        Save that of knowing that we do thy will,
        Through Jesus Christ our Lord.   Amen

"BOIL IN THE BAG" MEDITATION 27

As Head of Lower School, I spent part of each Wednesday lunchtime in the school library where I would supervise the pupils as they either read a book, or did their homework. Some of them came in regularly and one such lad was Kelvin, his favourite reading was science fiction, providing it was well illustrated with grotesque beings from outer space. He frequently drew some of these and then brought them along, so that I could share the delight in his latest 'find'. It therefore came as no surprise when, he suddenly appeared at my side book in hand. "Have you seen this one, sir?" he asked: but 'this one' was not his usual type of monster book at all, it was one by Cliff Richard - 'You, me and Jesus'. For once Kelvin had found a different story from outer space.

I like to feel, that what had prompted him to share his discovery with me was the fact that a short time before I had based my morning assembly on another book by Cliff - 'The way I see it'. I have a great admiration for this man, especially in the way that he is prepared to speak out for those things he believes in - even if they prove to be unpopular.

It was through my association with The Boys' Brigade, that I had the privilege of comparing three shows in which he played a leading role - two of these were at The Royal Albert Hall, where he was the Guest of Honour at the Annual Display. Most of the personalities that had appeared in this capacity, simple stood and gave a polite bow, or salute, to acknowledge the applause of the audience - not him - he jumped to his feet, arms held high, turning in all directions, loving every moment as the crowd showed their appreciation for his presence.

It was the third occasion, in 1972 at Wembley Arena, I remember most vividly. Basically it was a Boys' Show, but the programme included guest items such as the Band of The Royal Marines and, of course, Cliff. He was to appear immediately before the finale but was not due to arrive until after the show had started. Although I had prepared my introduction very carefully, I didn't know if he was prepared to do an encore, although I was sure the audience would want one. After his arrival I contacted his dressing room to clarify the situation. The answer surprised me. There would be no encore as this was essentially the boys' night, and he did not wish to steal the limelight. After his act had finished, I managed to make myself heard above the continued applause and went on to introduce the Finale. Cliff stayed on stage, and as a thirteen year old lad stepped forward to sing the closing hymn, he went forward to greet him and put him at his ease and remained there as the boy sung his solo. There was no arm waving this time, just a quiet, reverent respect for the talents of another.

The next year Cliff visited Bangladesh where he saw the work of Tear Fund in action. On this occasion he did not just stand back and show a quiet and reverent respect for the work of others, but started to actively associate himself with such work and has since made numerous visits of a similar kind to all parts of the world, as well as devoting the proceeds of his Gospel Concerts to finance this work of Christian love in action - work he promotes whenever he gets the chance.

Menu Master 28

Lent - Temptation

The English 'take away'

Reading - St Matthew 4 v 1 - 11

Then the Spirit led Jesus into the desert to be tempted by the Devil.
After spending forty days and forty nights without food, Jesus was hungry.
Then the Devil came to him and said, "If you are God's Son, order these
stones to turn into bread."

But Jesus answered, "The scripture says, 'Man shall not live on bread
alone, but needs every word that God speaks.'"

Hymns & Psalms 138

Seek ye first the kingdom of God,
  And his righteousness,
And all these things shall be added unto you:
  Allelu Alleluia.

Man shall live by bread alone,
  But by every word
That proceeds from the mouth of the Lord:
Allelu Alleluia.

Karen Lafferety
© 1972 Maranatha! Music Administered by Copycare Ltd.
Used by Permission

Prayer from the Companion to the Lectionary (Volume 3):
    Loving Father, we are so easily tempted, so fearful, so prone to lose our
courage.
    Sometimes we take the easy way out, allowing evil to triumph, shrinking
from action because we do not hold firmly to our beliefs.
    We complain about our suffering, which is as nothing in comparison with
that of your Son, our Saviour. Amen

© Copyright - Epworth Press; used by kind permission

"BOIL IN THE BAG" MEDITATION 28

On March 11th 1992 the Prime Minister, John Major, emerged from Number 10 Downing Street and announced that Parliament was to be dissolved the following Monday and a General Election would be held on Thursday April 9th. For several months the opposition parties had been asking for such an election but it was only the Prime Minister who could make such a decision, and now the general public had a decision to make too - who were they going to vote for? Strangely enough those decisions were taken during the period of Lent - the weeks leading up to Easter - a time in the Christian Church when people look at the decisions Jesus had to make when he was in the desert for forty days and forty nights but he did only what he believed was right and never took the easy way out.

Every day we are faced with some decision or other, most of them are easily made - what would you prefer for breakfast, cornflakes or cocopops? Where are you going on Saturday, football or ice skating? But there are times when the answers are not so easily found. Decisions that may have a great effect on our future - what kind of job do we want and are we prepared to carry on studying after we become sixteen? Are we going to listen to the opinions of others who are being rather critical about a close friend. If we are given a position of trust and responsibility - are we going to misuse that position for our own personal gain? Are we going to lie to get ourselves out of trouble and let someone else take the blame? Are we going to do what so called friends suggest, even though we know it is wrong, and could lead to serious trouble?

In August 1992 BBC 1 used its morning discussion programme to give teenagers a chance to express their views. It was called, 'Kids on Kilroy' - no connection with the expression we often find on walls - 'Kilroy wos 'ere' - but the title came from the name of the presenter, Robert Kilroy-Silk. One morning the audience expressed their views on friendship, gangs and bullying. Some very good ideas were put forward, but the one that made most sense was that the peer pressure to stay in the group - they did not like the word gang - only came if you were not prepared to conform to the pattern set by others. One of the examples they gave was that of smoking. If you are not prepared to smoke, you can't be one of us. Most youngsters experience such pressures and do things they would not normally do in order to keep the friendship of others.

At a time when teachers worked to rule - they would not cover the lessons of absent colleagues or those on strike - some pupils received only part-time education. Wondering what they did in their 'spare time', I asked one group how they occupied themselves on such occasions. The answer, "We go to Romford - to Debenhams - the take away store!" That needed no explanation - they were bored - so, as a group they went shoplifting. It started as a bit of fun - it developed into a dare - but it could finish with a court conviction. It's not always easy to decide what to do, but we must do what we believe is right, even if it that means loosing the friendship of someone we care about.

With such decisions, let your conscience be your guide.

Menu Master 29

Apathy

BBC Essex Community Help

Reading - John 19 v 17 - 24

He went out carrying his cross, and came to 'The Place of the Skull'. There they crucified him and also they crucified two other men one on each side, with Jesus between them. Pilate wrote a notice and had it put on the cross, 'Jesus of Nazareth the King of the Jews.' After the soldiers had crucified Jesus, they took his clothes and divided into four parts, one for each soldier. They also took the robe, which was made of woven cloth without any seams in it. The soldiers said one to another, "Let's not tear it: let's throw dice to see who will get it."

Hymns & Psalms 178

There is a green hill far away,
    outside a city wall,
Where the dear Lord was crucified,
    who died to save us all.

We may not know, we cannot tell,
    what pains he had to bear,
But we believe it was for us
    he hung and suffered there.
                    Cecil Frances Alexander (1818 - 95)

A Prayer - Eddie Espinosa (Let's Praise)

Change my heart, O God, make it ever true,
Change my heart, O God, may I be like you,
You are the potter, I am the clay,
    Mould me and make me,
    This is what I pray.   Amen
            Copyright © 1982 Mercy Publishing/Thankyou Music
            P.O. Box 75 Eastbourne, E. Sussex BN23 6NW
            For Europe only - used by permission

"BOIL IN THE BAG" MEDITATION 29

As I was preparing my notes for the earlier 'menus' on prejudice and understanding, the first line of a poem kept coming into my mind. I knew what the poem was about and I knew the name of the writer. The writer was G. A. Studdert-Kennedy, his name had stuck in my mind mainly because of his nickname - 'Woodbine Willie'. He had been a Padré in the First World War and had been given that name by the troops on the Western Front - in view of the fact he always carried a packet of Woodbine cigarettes in his pocket for the soldiers he met in the trenches. The words of his poem spoke of apathy and, in its way, this can often be far more hurtful than prejudice or a lack of understanding. What is worse than just being ignored?

After much searching I had failed to find the poem which started, 'When Jesus came to Westminster' - at least, that is what I thought. I mentioned my search for these words during a service I was taking at Chadwell-St-Mary and as we chatted over a cup of tea after the service one lady suggested she would write to her weekly magazine, they often found things like that for their readers. Her suggestion immediately made me think of an alternative - I could telephone the Community Help Line on BBC Essex Radio. The next day the call was made, that was on Monday August 12th 1991, and on the Tuesday morning an appeal was made, on my behalf, by Alison Hartley - but before Alison had a chance to give my telephone number the phone was ringing - naturally I thought it was impossible to get such a quick response, the number hadn't been given yet. I was wrong, for as I put the receiver to my ear I heard the familiar voice of Rev Anne Davies, the minister of our church. Anne informed me she had the very book I was looking for, but the line I mentioned was not 'When Jesus came to Westminster' but 'When Jesus came to Birmingham' - but then, as Anne suggested, it's the attitude that is important not the location. The Book was called 'The Unutterable Beauty' and the poem:-

'Indifference'

When Jesus came to Golgotha they hanged him on a tree,
They drave great nails through hands and feet, and made a Calvary.
They crowned him with a crown of thorns, red were his wounds and deep,
For those were crude and cruel days, and human flesh was cheap.

When Jesus came to Birmingham they simply passed him by,
They never hurt a hair of him, they only let him die.
For men had grown more tender, and they would not give him pain
They only just passed down the street and left him in the rain.

Still Jesus cried, "Forgive them, for they know not what they do,"
And still it rained the wintry rain that drenched Him through and through;
The crowds went home and left the streets without a soul to see
And Jesus crouched against a wall and cried for Calvary.

G. A. Studdert-Kennedy

Anne was right, the location in the first line was unimportant - the sentiment is expressed in the last line!

Menu Master 30

Mother's Day

Cashing in on the occasion

Reading - Isaiah 49 v 14 - 15

The people of Jerusalem said, "The Lord has abandoned us. He has forgotten us!" So the Lord answers, "Can a woman forget her own baby and not love the child she bore? Even if a mother should forget her child I will not forget you. Jerusalem I can never forget you! I have written your name on the palms of my hands."

Hymns & Psalms 367

Lord of the home, your only Son
 Received a mother's tender love
And from an earthly father won
 His vision of your home above.
Teach us to keep our homes so fair
 That, were our Lord a child once more,
He might be glad our hearth to share,
 And find a welcome at our door.
Albert F. Bayly (1901 -)
© *Copyright Oxford University Press, used by permission*

A Prayer of Thanksgiving (H&P 572 v 6) by Doreen Newport

Think of a world without any people,
 Think of a world with no one living there,
Think of a town without any houses,
 No one to love, and nobody to care:
We thank you, Lord, for families and friendships,
We thank you, Lord, and praise your holy name.
Amen
© *Stainer & Bell, used by permission*

"BOIL IN THE BAG" MEDITATION 30

The period leading up to Easter is called Lent, and the middle (or fourth) Sunday of Lent is commonly known as 'Mothers' Day'. This is no more than a commercial take over, bringing great financial gain to florists and card sellers. It started life in a completely different way, and although it was called Mothering Sunday, it had little to do with mothers. At the same time I am pleased there is a day on which we can show our appreciation to 'mum' - although it's a pity if we only do it once a year. On one occasion I was discussing with a group of youngsters what they were going to give to their mothers on the following Sunday; Joe, who was about fourteen, informed me he would give his mother a large box of chocolates and a card with a £10 note inside. I made the observation that either he was a very generous son or else he had a very co-operative father. Joe made it clear he would pay for the gifts himself - adding his weekend job was very profitable and he could afford it. When I asked where he worked, he told me he sold flowers outside a cemetery, there was no set price, the boss had told him to look at the customer and get as much as he could.

There was a time when Lent was strictly observed - a time of fasting and self-denial, but on one day, in the middle of Lent, feasting was permitted and those who usually met for worship in the small village chapels all went along to the Mother, or Parish, Church for a special celebration. Later, sometime in the eighteenth century, those working away from home were given time off so that they could return home, taking a present for their mothers and join in the special services. Today many churches hold a special service on Mothering Sunday and the children are given a small bunch of flowers to distribute to the ladies in the congregation or take them home to mum. Such a service takes us back to where it all started even if the purpose of the occasion has changed.

The Boys' Brigade always held a Church Parade on Mothers' Day at Riverview Church - each member was given a bunch of flowers to take home - in 1986 after the service, two of the boys, Tim and John, were walking past the church, not a flower in sight, a lady standing with me asked them what had happened to the flowers, the boys said nothing but turned to show they were in their back pockets - it's not easy to walk through the streets with a bunch of flowers when you are a teenager.

That's not the end of the story, for when I asked where they going (since they were now walking away from their homes), they said they were going to the shops to get some more flowers - they hadn't bought any themselves! I walked with them and took them home by car - you can't carry two bunches in your back pocket. As we drove along they asked, "May we come over to see you this afternoon?" I agreed. But it was only after we had had a meal and they had said goodbye that I realised the same two boys had done a similar thing the previous New Year's Eve - "May we come and see you?" That was just a few days after my mother had died. I believe they didn't want me to be alone. They showed concern, they showed they cared. That is what Mothers' Day should be about, not just flowers and expensive cards, but a practical expression of our feelings.

Menu Master 31

Conflict

Extracts from a diary

Reading - St Luke 22 39 - 46

Then he went off from them about the distance of a stone's throw, and knelt down and prayed. "Father," he said, "if you will, take this cup of suffering from me. Not my will, however, but your will be done."
An angel from heaven appeared to him, and strengthened him.
In great anguish he prayed even more fervently; his sweat was like great drops of blood falling to the ground.
Rising from his prayer, he went back to the disciples and found them asleep, worn out by their grief.

Hymn - Let's Praise - 47 (Dambusters March) Psalm 46

> God is our strength and refuge,
>   our present help in trouble;
> And we will not therefore fear
>   though the earth be changed.
> Though mountains shake and tremble,
>   though swirling floods are raging,
> God, the Lord of hosts is with us evermore.
> *Richard Bewes*
> © Copyright Richard Bewes / Jubilate Hymns - used by kind permission.

Prayer: Give us, O Father, your truth to tell us what we ought to believe and the decisions we ought to make, and give us your strength to make us able to face up to, and do the things which by ourselves we cannot do.
Amen.

"BOIL IN THE BAG" MEDITATION 31

Let me read a few extracts from my diary - in no special order

<u>Day 1</u> - Had set the alarm radio for an hour later than usual - yesterday had been a long and hectic day - woken up by telephone - unaware of the time - answered 'phone - caller said it was 7.25 am - and then asked, "Do you want a day's work, we are short staffed at school?" - I didn't really, but I went.

<u>Day 2</u> - Had been working on my book all day - at 10.15 pm felt like a break - it would be a quiet night at the club - took my notes to do a bit more work - as I walked along I felt inspired and wanted to write my thoughts down - as I entered the club the only person there said, "I'm so glad you've come in, I was hoping to find someone I could talk to!" - my thoughts had to wait until I got home.

<u>Day 3</u> - BBC 1 are showing Liverpool v Genoa (UEFA Cup) at the same time ITV are showing Spurs v Feyenoord (European Cup) - shall I record one and watch the other? My diary says 8pm Local Preachers Meeting at Wickford - went to meeting.

<u>Day 4</u> - yet again two good programmes on 'tele' - this time I could record one and watch the other - I had just started viewing when the 'phone rang - "May I come and see you?"

<u>Day 5</u> - having left the ironing for a few days I decided to get on with it - as I put the ironing board up I thought of an excellent theme for a service - ironing has still to be done.

These are not made up stories but actual incidents and underline the fact that we are constantly facing situations that cause conflict in our lives. You may feel they are fairly petty compared with the temptations and conflicts Christ had to face in the desert, but in some ways we face the same questions - getting our priorities right - how do we spend our time and the special talents we have been given - are we prepared to put friendship before personal preferences - why do we go to work (if only for the odd day) - is it for the money, or to use the skills we have been entrusted with?

All these 'instant conflicts' need an immediate reaction - there are of course much bigger situations and more complex situations - a career move - moving house - taking on greater responsibility - but hopefully we have more time to consider these, but decisions still have to be made. I live alone - my own master - how much more difficult it must be when there are two or three in the house and how more frequent the conflicts.

At the beginning of Lent we usually reflect on Christ's forty days in the wilderness - it still seems strange to consider an episode from the early days of Christ's ministry and to reflect on that period which comes so near to the end - but then he constantly met conflict all the time. The attitude of his mother and family when he left home to preach - the people he should choose to be his disciples - the constant opposition and arguments with the Pharisees - and what of the selected reading from St Luke's Gospel - this was the hardest decision of all but he still said, "Your will be done."

Menu Master 32

Palm Sunday

F A Cup Winners

Reading - St Matthew 21 v 1 - 11

As Jesus and his disciples approached Jerusalem, they came to Bethphage at the Mount of Olives. There Jesus sent two his disciples on ahead with these instructions, "Go the village there ahead of you, and at once you will find a donkey tied up with her colt beside her. Untie them and bring them to me. And if anyone says anything, tell him, 'The Master needs them; and they will let them go at once.' So the disciples did as Jesus had told them. They took the donkey and the colt, threw their cloaks over them, and Jesus got on. Others cut branches from the trees and spread them on the road and as they walked in front of him, they began to shout, "Praise to David's Son! God bless him who comes in the name of the Lord!"

Hymns & Psalms 162

> Trotting, trotting through Jerusalem,
> Jesus sitting on a donkey's back,
> Children waving branches, singing:
> 'Happy is he that comes in the name of the Lord!'
> *Eric Reid (1936 - 70)*
> *© Copyright Stainer & Bell, used by permission*

Prayer: As we look at the stories of Jesus, O Father, we realise there were times when he was very happy and there were times when he was very sad. There were times when he was cheered - there were times when he was jeered. Yet, whatever the circumstances - whatever the reactions of his followers - he realised that he was not alone, but you were with him, to share his happiness and to help and strengthen him through the more difficult times. So, O Father, be with us and help us to know you are with us always. We ask this, in his name.   Amen

"BOIL IN THE BAG" MEDITATION 32

It has all become an essential part of F A Cup Final to parade the Cup with the winning team the following day. As they ride in triumph on an open top bus through the streets of their town or city they are cheered and greeted by thousands of fans. In 1988 Wimbledon won the cup, having beaten the famous Liverpool. As the bus went on its journey, there was a large banner across the road - 'Wimbledon twinned with Lourdes'. On Palm Sunday we recall another triumphal entry into a large city - it was not the triumphal entry of a team, but of one man, a man who although he hadn't won a trophy, he had won the hearts of the people - and the welcome was just as great. Many have retold the story of this great event but the one I like best is that told by David Kossoff during a radio broadcast in 1963.

It was a story about three donkeys. They had met in heaven and found that they had quite a lot in common. All three had lived and worked in the same part of the same country nearly two thousand years ago. The first donkey had told of a baby born in a stable and how shepherds and wise men had visited him. The second told of a boy from Nazareth who called the temple in Jerusalem, 'my father's house'. Now it was the turn of the third donkey to tell his story. He also knew the Temple well, having lived all his life in Jerusalem. When he was around it was more a kind of covered market than a house of prayer. He recalleed that there was nearly a riot there one day when a young preacher and his followers overturned all the stalls and threw everybody out. That young preacher got himself into a right lot of trouble.

Having come to Jerusalem that morning; two of his friends had gone to the yard where the donkey lived: he was only young, didn't even have a saddle, had never been ridden, a bit wild. These two took him to the young preacher and put clothes across his back. He didn't like it and started to play up but the young preacher put his hand on him and, it was all right. He got on the donkey's back and off they went. He must have been very famous, there never saw such crowds. They loved him! They threw their cloaks on the road and spread leafy branches so the donkey could walk softly. They called him king and prophet and son of David. Fantastic noise. He had dismounted at the temple and started throwing out all the traders. He made more enemies than friends. He was dead by the end of the week! But before that happened, after he cleared the temple, he stayed there and lots of sick people came to him and he healed them. It was then the Romans took a hand and he was sentenced to death. The donkey remembered carrying dozens up to Golgotha where he was crucified.

As he died the skies went dark so the donkey had run for his life. That evening he had to go back again. A rich man from a place called Arimathea hired him to carry the young preacher's body to a sort of tomb cut in the rock. The Romans sealed it with a huge rock, and put a guard of soldiers there as well. Saturday was a quiet, sad day. Very early the next morning his master handed him over to two women. One rode on his back and the other led him. The third donkey then concluded his story by saying, "Now, I don't ask you to believe this, but, when we got there, there were no guards, the great stone was rolled to one side, and the tomb, which seemed filled with light, was empty!"

Menu Master 33

Maundy Thursday

A strange greeting

Reading - St John 13 v 2 - 15

'Jesus rose from the table, took off his outer garment, and tied a towel round his waist. Then he poured some water into a basin and began to wash the disciples' feet and dry them with the towel. Jesus went on to say, "I have set an example for you, so that you will do just what I have done for you. Now you know this truth, how happy you will be if you put it into practice."

Hymns & Psalms 145

Kneels at the feet of his friends,
Silently washes their feet,
Master who acts as a slave to them.
  Jesu, Jesu,
    Fill us with your love,
    Show us how to serve
The neighbours we have from you.
T.S. Colvin (1925 -)

Prayer: Help us to remember the act of service and devotion undertaken by Jesus. Let us not think too highly of ourselves but remember his lesson in humility, so that we may always be ready to care about and serve others and in so doing, we may serve you.   Amen

"BOIL IN THE BAG" MEDITATION 33

Normally when you are welcomed into a home or attend a special function you are greeted with a handshake. I wonder how you would react if they didn't shake your hand, but washed it instead? That was the experience of Janet Hodgson when she attended the World Methodist Conference in Kenya. Janet and her party had travelled many miles from Nairobi and as they left the coach, they felt hot and sticky and ready for a meal. They went into a hut where the meal had been prepared but as they entered, one of the Kenyan ladies had a kettle full of water and a bowl, and as each person passed her, she washed their hands. Recalling this incident Janet goes on to explain how she was immediately reminded of that act of service and devotion when Jesus washed his disciples' feet, and for the first time she felt very close to understanding what that really meant.

That is the reading associated with this particular menu - and, to put it in the right context, it happened on the day before Jesus was crucified - in other words the day before Good Friday or, as we now call it, Maundy Thursday. That word 'Maundy' is a very interesting one. It comes from the Latin word 'mandatum' meaning 'command'. Jesus said, "A new commandment I give you, love one another, as I have loved you." Most people think of 'Maundy' in connection with money - this is because ever since 1689 the monarch has distributed specially minted coins to the poor on Maundy Thursday. There was a time when this always took place in Westminster Abbey but now it happens in various cathedrals throughout the country. It is worth noting that this custom was actually started in the fourteenth century by King Edward III, but he did not distribute money, he washed and kissed the feet of the poor, (although it is true to say they had already been washed by the Yeomen of the Laundry before the monarch arrived). At least we can see where the custom started and even today the clergy present at the ceremony still carry linen towels on their shoulders to remind people of the original custom.

During their holidays some people are lucky enough to stay in a hotel where everything is done for them - for many others, home is just like that, they are waited on hand and foot - but let us remember there are those who deliberately give up their holidays - and pay their own expenses - to take others away and look after them in many different ways, such as organising an interesting programme, preparing the meals and, in the case of handicapped people, who would not get a holiday otherwise, wash, dress and feed them as well. I wonder how many members of the uniformed organisations realise the sacrifices their leaders make in order that may attend an annual camp or go on a weekend expedition - the same applies to school trips with staff who are on duty twenty fours a day - but they do it because they care about those they take, they want to help them get the opportunities they might otherwise miss.

'I'm in the boat, Jack' is a phrase not often heard these days, but it means looking after yourself and not bothering about the needs of others, in other words, being selfish. Greater satisfaction can often be found in showing concern for the needs of others.

Menu Master 34

Good Friday

Wells Cathedral

Reading - St Luke 22 v 54 -62

When one of the servant girls saw Peter sitting there at the fire, she looked straight at him and said, "This man too, was with Jesus!" But Peter denied it, "Woman, I don't even know him!" After a little while a man noticed Peter and said, "You are one of them, too!" But Peter answered and said, "Man, I am not!"

And about an hour later another man insisted strongly, "There isn't any doubt that this man was with Jesus, because he also is a Galilean!" But Peter answered, "I don't know what you are talking about!"

At once, while he was still speaking, a cock crowed.

Hymns & Psalms 180

When I survey the wondrous cross,
  On which the Prince of Glory died
My richest gain I count but loss,
  And pour contempt on all my pride.
Isaac Watts (1674-1748)

Prayer: We thank you for the life of Jesus, his ministry, his words and his example. We thank you too, that when the time came, he bravely faced a cruel death to show his great love for all mankind. Help us to see how, through that sacrifice of love, we can come to know the real meaning of life, and that something of his sacrifice, and his love, can be seen in the way we live. For his sake.   Amen

"BOIL IN THE BAG" MEDITATION 34

"War can be a very impersonal, one feels no involvement."
That statement was made by a headmaster who had returned from Kuwait just before it was invaded by Iraq in 1990. He then went on to say that was the way he had felt until he heard a news broadcast in which it was stated "one of the first civilian casualties, killed by the Iraqis, was Douglas McCrosskey." At that moment his attitude changed completely; he had dined with Douglas the night before he returned home.

To many, Easter is just like that, it is impersonal, there is no involvement, and unfortunately their attitude never changes - since they have had no personal experience to make it do so.

One of the saddest stories I ever heard was that of a small girl in the East End of London who had been given a gold cross and chain for her birthday; as one of her friends admired it, she was heard to say, "Yes, and there's a little man on it. I wonder who he is?" She knew even less than a small boy from the same area who, when asked what he knew about Jesus, simply replied, "D'y mean that bloke who 'as 'is name on churches?"

In 1991 I was watching the Good Friday television programme from Wells Cathedral. As an introduction the presenter talked to some of the people passing by and he put the same question to each: "What does Good Friday mean to you?" The first was a young man in his early twenties, and he answered, "It gives me another day with me bird." He had a little more success with a middle aged lady who said, "Well it's about him ... you know ... him ... Christ and ... and all that!" How difficult it was for her to mention His name. There were two teenagers who were walking along together, one replied by saying, "It's the day you have fish and chips." The other, however, gave a much fuller answer, "It was the day Jesus died on a cross, he was placed in a tomb, that belonged to someone else and then on the third day he rose again." Unfortunately the whole thing was then completely ruined for me, when his friend who had been looking on in amazement. asked, "Where did you learn all that then?" And the answer, "I took RE in my GCSE, didn't I."

Jesus, to that young man, and to many others as well, is just a figure in a book. The whole thing is so impersonal, nothing to do with them really. It's bad enough at Christmas, when people fail to get involved with what that's all about, but at least they seem to know the story - maybe it's because we send cards and the Nativity scene is on many of them. Few people send cards at Easter in that way - Easter is just a time for 'eggs' and 'flowers', or an extra couple of days with 'the bird'. Now go back to the story of that first Good Friday, was the pattern any different then? Who really wanted to get involved when the going got tough? Where were his friends when he needed them most? Even Peter, 'the rock', the one on whom Jesus said he would build his church, failed to come up to expectations and, on three separate occasions, denied that he had any association with Jesus. Then again, is that why so many don't want to get involved in the first place? They are frightened of the consequences!

Menu Master 35

Easter Day

Concern for the individual

Reading - St John 20 v 1 - 16

Mary stood crying outside the tomb. While she was still crying, she bent over and looked in the tomb and saw two angels there dressed in white, sitting where the body of Jesus had been. "Woman, why are you crying?" they asked her. She answered, "They have taken my Lord away, and I do not know where they have put him!" Then she turned round and saw Jesus standing there: but she did not know that it was Jesus. "Woman, why are you crying?" Jesus asked her. "Who is it you are looking for?" She thought it was the gardener, so she asked him, "If you took him away, sir, tell me where you have put him, and I will go and get him." Jesus said to her, "Mary."

Hymns & Psalms 190 (Tune Truro)

> Christ is alive! Let Christians sing;
>   The cross stands empty to the sky;
> Let streets and homes with praises ring;
>   Love, drowned in death, shall never die.
>   *Brian Wren*
>   © *reprinted by permission of Oxford University Press*

Prayer: We give you thanks and praise, O Father, for the glorious resurrection of your Son. Help us, to show our praise, not merely with words alone, but with deeds and actions that reflect the life and attitude of him who was dead, but was raised again, and may we ever be faithful in and through all that we do.
In the name of Jesus, our Risen Lord.   Amen

"BOIL IN THE BAG" MEDITATION 35

Each of the Gospel writers tells, in his own way, the story of the day that started in such a dramatic way, and has become the most memorable day in life of the Christian Church. These stories are not contradictory in their content, they are complementary, together they give us a more complete picture of all that happened. Not only do they complement one another, they also complement earlier stories in the life of Christ. At the beginning of his ministry, Jesus made it very clear he would do nothing spectacular to impress people, or persuade them to his way of life and thinking. He would not misuse or abuse his great power. Now, as we consider his resurrection, the pattern is still the same, it was an earth shattering event and yet there were no great crowds to witness it. To begin with the revelation only came to those who were closest to him, and even they did not appreciate, at first, what was really happening. Yet, alongside this fact, there is another, and this shows us one of the most important aspects of the Christ's attitude to people, and the Easter story only serves to underline it - Christ's concern was for the individual, and what was true some two thousand years ago, is as true today.

Mark tells of a messenger who said, "Go and tell my disciples, including Peter." This is very interesting since the other writers do not mention Peter by name - does this mean Mark had access to privileged information? Yes he did. Towards the end of his life, Peter was often accompanied by Mark and he must have given him a great deal of the material that became a part of his gospel. Why should Peter be singled out in this way? Simply because Peter had let Jesus down badly - he had denied Jesus three times and felt dreadful when he realised what he had done - Jesus wanted to reassure him all was well. That same reassurance was also given to Mary.

There are several 'Marys' connected with this story, but the one who reached the tomb first, the one who received the message so early that Sunday morning, was Mary Magdalene. Like Peter, she must have felt so desperate at that time since Jesus had been the only person to really understand her and he had completely changed her life. She wanted to be near him, even if he was dead. Then, as she stayed near to the tomb, a most remarkable thing happened; through her tears, she saw what she thought to be a gardener, and even spoke to him as such. It was only when Jesus addressed her by name that she realised he was still alive. One cannot appreciate the emotion of that moment when Jesus simply said, "Mary!" All through his life Jesus had constantly shown his concern for, and his understanding of the individual - now that he 'has been raised' - that same sense of caring, that same concern for, and understanding of, each and every individual is even greater.

In 'The Trial Of Jesus' there is a striking passage in which Longinus, the Roman centurion in command of the soldiers at the Cross, comes back to Pilate and hands in his report on the day's work. The report is given, when Procula, Pilate's wife asks "Do you think He is dead?" "No lady," he replies, "I don't." "Then where is He?" "Let loose in the world lady, where neither Roman nor Jew can stop His truth."

THE THIRD COURSE

(Summer Term)

"BOIL IN THE BAG" MEDITATIONS

Summer Term   May - July

Menu Master 36

The road to Emmaus

Footprints

Reading - St Luke 24 v 13 - 35

That same day two of Jesus' followers were going to a village named Emmaus, about eleven kilometres from Jerusalem and they were talking about all the things that had happened. As they talked Jesus himself drew near and walked along with them; they saw him, but somehow did not recognise him. As they came near to the village to which they were going, Jesus acted as if he were going farther; but they held him back saying, "Stay with us, the day is almost over." He sat down to eat with them, took the bread and said the blessing. Then their eyes were opened and they recognised him.

Hymns & Psalms 645

> Perchance we have not always known
>   Who has been with us by the way,
> Amid day's uproar we have missed
>   Some word that thou hast had to say.
> In silent night, O Saviour dear,
> We would not fail thy voice to hear.
> *James Ashcroft Noble (1844-96)*

Prayer: Forgive us, Lord Jesus, because so often, like your followers of old, we find it difficult to understand the Easter story. We find it difficult to realise that you are still at work in the world, even if we cannot see you.
Come to us in your risen power and take away all our doubts and fears, so that our faith may be that much stronger.   Amen

Most of those connected with the Easter story are well known people - such as Peter, Judas and Mary - the exception is a man named Cleopas. All we know about him is that he was a follower of Jesus who was returning to his home in Emmaus on the Sunday after the crucifixion. He was not alone for there is also mention of a travelling companion, most people believe this was another man, but I see no reason why it could not have been his wife. In any case as they walked along they were joined by a third person, one who realised their obvious sadness and tried to comfort them by explaining the reasons for Jesus' death. What they didn't realise was that this person was Jesus himself. It was only when they invited the stranger in for a meal that they recognised him as he took the bread, broke it and gave thanks.

When you look back at the contents of the previous 'menu' this again emphasises Jesus' concern for the individual - he is closest to us when we need him most and we don't always appreciate it or understand what he is trying to do to help us. Leonard Cheshire was a famous airman in the in the Second World War; up to that time his whole life had been very successful but strangely enough when the war was over he found it hard to find something to do, something that is with a real purpose - he was not looking for something that was Christian based for he had made up his mind there was no God. He tried going into business but that was unsuccessful. It was at that time he went to see Arthur Dykes who was dying of cancer. Arthur had no friends and no home. By taking him to his home and looking after him he realised this dying man had something to offer him - it was his deep faith and belief in God. As a result of their meeting Leonard Cheshire not only found a purpose in life, he also found a deep faith and today there are many Cheshire Homes not only in Britain but all over the world.

That 'Road to Emmaus Experience' is reflected in the story 'Footprints'

> *One night a man had a dream. He dreamed he was walking along the beach with the Lord. Across the sky flashed scenes from his life.*
>
> *For each scene he noticed two sets of footprints in the sand, one belonging to him - the other, to the Lord.*
>
> *When the last scene of his life flashed before him, he looked back at his footprints in the sand and noticed that many times along the path of his life there was only one set of footprints.*
>
> *He also noticed that it happened at the very lowest and saddest times of his life. This really bothered him and he questioned the Lord about it, "Lord, you once said that if I decided to follow you, you'd walk with me all the way. Now I notice that during the most troublesome times in my life, there is only one set of footprints. I don't understand why, when I need you most, you would leave me."*
>
> *The Lord replied, "My precious child, I love you, and I would never leave you. During the times of trial and suffering, when you see only one set of footprints in the sand, it was then that I carried you."*

Menu Master 37

Forgiveness

Simon Johnson

Reading - St John 21 v 15 - 19

After they had eaten, Jesus said to Simon Peter, "Simon, son of John, do you love me more than these others do?" "Yes Lord," he answered, "you know that I love you." Jesus said to him, "Take care of my lambs." A second time Jesus said to him, "Simon, son of John, do you love me?" "Yes, Lord," he answered, "you know that I love you." Jesus said to him, "Take care of my sheep." A third time Jesus said, "Simon son of John, do you love me." Peter was sad when the question was asked for the third time.

Hymns & Psalms 521

Hark my soul! It is the Lord;
'Tis thy Saviour, hear his word:
Jesus speaks, and speaks to thee;
'Say, poor sinner, lov'st thou me?'

Lord, it is my chief complaint
That my love is weak and faint:
Yet I love thee, and adore,
O for grace to love thee more!
William Cowper (1731-1800)

A prayer of St Augustine:
O Thou, from whom to be turned, is to fall,
to whom to be turned, is to rise,
and in whom to stand, is to abide forever.
Grant us in all our duties, thy help,
in all our perplexities, thy guidance,
in all our dangers, thy protection,
and in all our sorrows thy peace.
Through Jesus Christ our Lord.   Amen

"BOIL IN THE BAG" MEDITATION 37

There are times in life when things just don't plan out in the way we expected they would - we are faced with some great disappointment or even tragedy - how do we react? Some become dispirited and 'go into their shell', as we say - others accept the situation and try to get on with life as best they can. There are experiences that come to us all - it may be something quite small (although it doesn't appear like that at the time), being dropped from the football team or losing the friendship of someone we cared about - other circumstances are far more difficult for us to face up to, the loss of a job, the loss of a parent. Somehow life must go on and it is no good just sitting back and moping about it - that only makes matters worse. I can still vividly remember, although it happened over thirty years ago, sitting with my mother watching television, waiting for the 1961 Cup Final to start, the crowd were singing 'Abide with me' when a telegram arrived telling us my mother's sister, a favourite aunt of mine, had died in hospital - it was not unexpected news but when it happened we were shattered. But life had to go on and we had to help and support each other.

I wonder how the disciples must have felt when they realised Jesus was dead? The reality was that he was no longer with them. I know he appeared to them again on that Easter Day, but the whole thing was not easy for them to accept or understand. At first they were too scared to come from behind locked doors but eventually they tried to face up to the situation and face the world again, it was then Jesus appeared to his disciples again. Like many of us when faced with tragedy or disaster, we simply say to ourselves, 'life must go on', and get back to whatever we were doing. That is what the disciples did. For some of them, they went back to the one job they knew - and it was Peter who suggested, "I am going fishing." Back to square one. They fished all night - they caught nothing - they must have felt really down. Then at the moment when they were at their lowest and coming back to the shore feeling completely fed up, Jesus was there with them - but they failed to recognise him, the truth only dawned when he told them to cast their nets again and this time they caught more fish than they imagined possible.

As they had a meal together Jesus came straight to the point, turning to Peter, he said, "Simon, son of John, do you love me more than these others do?" "Yes Lord," he answered, "you know that I love you." Jesus said to him, "Take care of my lambs." Such a question was put not once, not twice, but three times. That must have hurt Peter, three times he had denied Jesus and three times the question was put, but look how Jesus addressed him, 'Simon, son of John.' Jesus had gone back to his original name. That hurt as well. Life must go on, but not in the way he had thought it would - not back to square one, alone and with little purpose in life, now he had a new commission - in fact he had two commissions - to be a 'fisher of men' and to 'care for the sheep' - witnessing and caring.

It is a fact of life that we often learn more from our failures than from our successes. What's more, difficult circumstances can bring us to a greater understanding of Jesus and, although we have done wrong, Jesus does not hold it against us if we are truly sorry for what we have done.

Menu Master 38

For those starting out to work.

Tens and units

Reading - St Matthew 7 v 24 - 29

So then, anyone who hears these words of mine and obeys them is like a wise man who built his house on rock. But anyone who hears these words of mine and does not obey them is like a foolish man who built his house on sand.

Hymns & Psalms 746

One more step along the world I go,
One more step along the world I go,
From the old things to the new
Keep me travelling along with you.

And it's from the old I travel to the new;
Keep me travelling along with you.
Sydney Carter (1915 -)
© *Copyright, Stainer & Bell Ltd., used by permission.*

Prayer: Help us, O Lord, to get the 'tens and units' right in our life - so that we may know the difference between what is right and what is wrong.
Help us to spend our time wisely and not waste it on things that do not matter - may we be considerate and not selfish, honest and not underhanded in our dealings with other people, so that we can go about without a guilty conscience - building only on a solid foundation as Jesus suggested.
We ask this our prayer in his name.   Amen.

A class of pupils were asked to find the answer to the simple question - multiply thirteen by seven. The first answer offered was twenty eight. The boy who had provided this answer was now invited to show his working on the blackboard - his solution was like this -

```
        7
  x   13
      ----
      21
       7
      ----
      28
      ----
```

Two mistakes of course - why use long multiplication; and if you do what about the nought? The teacher tried to help him by asking, "What do we mean by seven thirteens?" The boy gave the correct answer this time, saying, "Seven lots of thirteen added together." He was then asked to work that out and he wrote the number '13' seven times, one under the other - and proceeded to add them up - "Three, six, nine, twelve, fifteen, eighteen, twenty one, - going well, right so far, but then he continued, as he turned his attention to the other column twenty two, twenty three, twenty four, twenty five, twenty six, twenty seven, twenty eight!!

The teacher was not finished. She then tried a different approach by asking him, "So what will you get if you divide twenty eight by seven? The lad looked very thoughtful and then replied, "Thirteen Miss!" Again he was asked to explain how he had found such an answer.

This was his method, he had started with long multiplication, so now he tried long division - with the result -

```
7 ) 28    seven into two won't go, try seven into eight
          that goes once and one over -        1
          so we get                       7 ) 28
```

the one over goes with the two to give twenty one and seven into twenty one goes three times - answer - '13'!
What that boy did in maths, so many do in life - mix up the tens and units. They have a wrong sense of values.

In their opinion it doesn't matter if you tell lies, providing it keeps you out of trouble. "I'm sorry I couldn't come to football practice, I had too much homework to do." What they really meant was, their 'homework' was called Karen, she was a very attractive fifteen year old with long blonde hair. Then there are those who believe that there is nothing wrong with stealing. They don't call it stealing they just find it before it's really lost, something that doesn't belong to them and they keep it without trying to find the owner. In their opinion the person who lost it should have been more careful in looking after their property. Mind you, the moment they lose something themselves, they immediately suggest it has been stolen - even if they have just forgotten where they left it. Lying and stealing are two of the commonest ways in which we can have a wrong sense of values.

Menu Master 39

Understanding

A Senior Citizen Defined

Reading - St Matthew 22 v 34 - 40

Jesus answered, "'Love the Lord your God with all your heart, with all your soul and with all your mind.' This is the greatest and most important commandment. The second most important commandment is like it, 'Love your neighbour as you love yourself.' The whole Law of Moses and the teachings of the prophets depend on these two commandments."

Hymns & Psalms 802 (v 2)

Teach me thy patience; still with thee
In closer, dearer company,
  In work that keeps faith sweet and strong,
  In trust that triumphs over wrong,
In hope that sends a shining ray
Far down the future's broadening way.
  In hope that only thou canst give,
  With thee, O Master, let me live.
Washington Gladden (1836-1918)

Prayer   Help us, O Lord, to realise different people have been brought up in different ways - maybe they have a different sense of values, a different view on life because the world of their childhood was not the world of ours - help us to show consideration and understanding towards them. Amen

"BOIL IN THE BAG" MEDITATION 39

As soon as people speak of prejudice or intolerance - in other words a lack of understanding or a lack of sympathy with the views of others - they associate such things with racial or religious differences. Ask a number of selected people if they had ever found themselves discriminated against - would the Christian have the same opinions as the Jew, would an Englishman have the same opinions as a West Indian? I doubt it, but these are the ones we think of in such matters. Now let us think of two others, and ask the same question - do teenagers feel they are discriminated against - do old aged pensioners? I believe these people sometimes think they are. I wonder why? Look at this humorous, but true definition of a senior citizen.

> A senior citizen is one who was here before the pill, television, frozen foods, credit cards and ballpoint pens.
> For them, time sharing meant being together.
> There were no computers, so a chip meant a piece of wood or a fried potato, hardware meant durable, software did not exist and porn meant going to 'uncle's' for a loan.
> They were before pantihose, dishwashers, tumble dryers, drip dry and electric blankets.
> Teenagers never wore jeans but girls had Peter Pan collars and thought that cleavage was something the butcher did.
> They got married first and lived together afterwards - how quaint can one be?
> They were before Batman, vitamin pills, disposable nappies, instant coffee, pizzas and Chinese takeaways.
> In their day smoking was fashionable but grass was for mowing and pot was a cooking utensil.
> As for gay people, they were the life and soul of the party - while aids meant beauty treatment or help for those in trouble.
> When you think about it senior citizens must be a hardy bunch to have survived and made all those adjustments in a world where there has been so many changes.

I wonder if the lack of understanding and intolerance is found not so much between the various religions or nationalities - we only have to look at relationships in an international camp to see that - I believe the greatest lack of understanding and the greatest lack of tolerance is found between those of the same religion or nationality but of varying age groups. Put yourself in someone else's shoes. Someone who is younger or older than you, do you try to understand the way in which they were brought up. For the elderly the world has changed a great deal. How different their world, from the world of the teenager of today, when for many the bedroom has become a vast collection of technological equipment, a colour TV and a video recorder, a computer parents cannot understand and the noise from a hi-fi stack that no one seems to understand. Standards have changed and values are different but each must try to understand the world of the other. As the theme tune of that popular soap puts it, 'Neighbours, everybody needs good neighbours, with a little understanding ...' and, after all, understanding does not always mean accepting. With a little understanding there would be fewer arguments in the family.

Menu Master 40

Whitsun

Confusion

Reading - Acts 2 v 1 - 8

When the day of Pentecost came, all the believers were gathered together in one place. Suddenly there was a noise from the sky which sounded like a strong wind blowing, and it filled the whole house where they were sitting. Then they saw what looked like tongues of fire which spread out and touched each person there. They were all filled with the Holy Spirit and began to talk in other languages, as the Spirit enabled them to speak.

Hymns & Psalms 312

Our blest Redeemer, ere he breathed
His tender last farewell,
A Guide, a Comforter bequeathed,
With us to dwell.
He came in tongues of living flame,
To teach, convince, subdue;
All-powerful as the wind he came,
As viewless too.
Henriette Auber (1773-1862)

Prayer:

Holy Spirit, giver of Life and light
Impart to us thoughts higher than our own,
prayers better than our own,
and power beyond our own power,
so we may spend and be spent
in your ways of love and goodness,
and so be more like Jesus Christ. Amen

"BOIL IN THE BAG" MEDITATION 40

In April 1971 The London Borough of Havering was twinned with the German town of Ludwigshafen-am-Rhein. Brittons School had been invited to twin with the Anne Frank Realschule and pupil exchange visits be arranged. These visits would be during the school holidays so that the pupils and staff did not miss valuable term time, with the German party coming to England at Easter - and the English party travelling at Whitsun. Such an arrangement also allowed those taking part to spend some time in the school of their hosts. Within days of the charter being signed the first pupils from Ludwigshaven arrived in Havering and the visit proved to be very successful, as did the visit of the English party to Germany when they took the school band to give a series of concerts. Similar arrangements were made for the following year when a school choir would come to Havering and the band would once again travel to the Rhine. The Easter-Whitsun exchange was established.

Plans for the following year seemed to be going smoothly, the Easter visit had proved to be even more popular, with both hosts and guests having a most enjoyable time, but three weeks before the Brittons School party were due to leave, a small boy approached the teacher responsible for the organisation at that end, and asked, "When is it we are going to Germany, sir?" The teacher was quite surprised, realising the number of letters and information sheets that had been distributed. As the conversation continued it became apparent that the boy thought he knew the date - 26th May - but his German friend had written to say he was expecting him on 19th and to make matters worse he was soon joined by another pupil who had received a similar letter. Correspondence between the two schools was carefully checked and there was no doubt that the letters stated clearly the 26th. It was then realised that the friends in Germany had failed to check these dates, they had thought only of a Whitsun visit, after all that was the arrangement, but unfortunately that was also the year - 1972 - that government legislation had introduced the 'Spring Bank Holiday' which was to take the place of the traditional Whit Monday. Spring Bank Holiday was on May 29th - Whit Sunday May 21st. A church festival had been replaced by a public holiday - surprisingly many people still refer to the Spring Bank Holiday as Whitsun but the two things are completely different and the dates rarely coincide.

Most diaries give the alternative name for this Church Festival - they call it 'Pentecost'. There are ten days after Ascension Day, which is forty days after the Feast of the Passover (Easter); so there are fifty days between Easter and Pentecost (a Jewish harvest festival) - the name comes from the Greek 'pentekoste' and Latin 'pentecoste' - both mean fiftieth. Jesus had told his disciples to go and teach all nations - not an easy thing to do, realising the great opposition to such work, but it was during this festival that they received the power to be able do so - the gift of the Holy Spirit. A certain advert claims their lager can 'reach those parts others cannot' - there is no proof of such a miracle but there is tremendous evidence for the claims of the Holy Spirit. His power changed timid men into bold ones no longer hiding behind locked doors but speaking openly of what they believed.

Menu Master 41

The Trinity - 1

On writing a book

Reading - John 14 v 15 - 26

If you love me, you will obey my commandments. I will ask the Father, and he will give you another Helper, who will stay with you for ever. He is the Spirit who reveals the truth about God.

I have told you this while I am still with you. The Helper, the Holy Spirit, whom the Father will send in my name will teach you everything and make you remember all that I have told you.

Hymns & Psalms 578 (a suggested verse 4)

Peace of the dove, peace of the dove,
Bringing God's good news,
Bringing God's good news.
Power of the wind, power of the wind,
Blowing where it will, blowing where it will,
Burning of fire makes us clean and new,
Symbols of love and the promise true;
Spirit of God, Spirit of God, be upon us now.

Prayer: O God, our Father, help us to show a greater interest in the reading of your word, and help us to read it with understanding.
Give us an even greater understanding as we see the thoughts and truths it contains reflected in the life of your Son, who was also called The Word.
Thus, may your Holy Spirit, so govern and direct us, that the pattern of our lives will reflect only the life of him in whose name we ask this prayer. Amen

"BOIL IN THE BAG" MEDITATION 41

Every school has at least one teacher who, given the opportunity, gets away from the subject he should be teaching and starts talking about his own particular pet interest - I well remember one like that - he had just left the RAF and was forever telling us about radar - needless to say we played up to this, and gave him every opportunity we could. I now find that some of my ex-pupils tell me how easy it was to get me 'off the subject' too - usually they were not very subtle in the way they did it either - 'Did you see the match last night, sir?' - 'Is you band playing this weekend?' They knew, and I knew they knew, these were two of my interests - what they failed to realise was that very often I was looking for such an opportunity - there were times when I too wanted a break from mathematics - and I loved telling stories.

It was this love of telling stories that helped me make up my mind to write this book. The idea had been there for years, but an idea is one thing - carrying it out is another. It was only during retirement that I found the time to do it, but then came the task of selecting the right stories and presenting them in such a way that they did the job I intended them to do. Putting my ideas into words to get my message across. In a strange kind of way that is why Jesus was born - for many years God had tried to get his ideas across - 'he spoke through the prophets', telling men how he wanted them to live, how they should get their priorities right and trust him to help them. They listened but seldom took the advice, they preferred their own judgement and usually managed to make a right mess of things.

When John wrote his gospel he told the story of the birth of Jesus, but, unlike the others, he told it in a completely different way. They talked about shepherds, wise men, and a baby in a stable - John referred to Jesus as 'The Word' - the word who came to the people and at first they never recognised him or accepted him for what he was. In that sense, God was putting his ideas into words, is a bit like me writing a book - trying to get my point across - presenting my ideas in such a way that people can understand - at least I hope they can. God went one better, illustrating his thinking with an audio-visual aid - if I can refer to Jesus in such a way - but in a real sense that is just what he was. God was saying, this is how I want you to live, this is the perfect example - one who cares about all kinds of people, one who trusts, one who loves - and is even prepared to die to show such trust and love. God the Father sent his Son.

The remarkable thing is Jesus left nothing for his followers in writing, yet we still know what he said and what he did nearly two thousand years later. Let's go back to the idea of my book - after it was written, the hardest part was still to come - I had to find a publisher so that others could read it. We often refer to God as 'The Trinity' - God the Father, God the Son, and God the Holy Spirit. It was the Holy Spirit who gave men and women the ability - the courage and the strength not only to live as God had told them, but to write about it and be prepared to tell others about the way Jesus had lived and what he had said - the Holy Spirit was the Publisher for God's Word.

Menu Master 42

The Trinity - 2

On giving instruction

Reading - Acts 2 v 22 - 24 & 32 - 36

Jesus of Nazareth was a man whose divine authority was clearly proven to you by all the miracles and wonders God performed through him. God raised this very Jesus from death, and we are all witnesses to this fact. He has been raised to right-hand side of God his Father, and received from him the Holy Spirit, as he had promised. What you now see and hear is his gift that he has poured out on us.

Hymns & Psalms 7

Holy, holy, holy, Lord God Almighty!
  Early in the morning our song shall rise to thee
Holy, holy, holy, merciful and mighty,
  God in Three Persons, blessed Trinity!
Reginald Heber (1783-1826)

Prayer: God the Father, you created the universe, you made us in your own image, you sent your Son, Jesus Christ to be our Saviour.
We worship and adore you.
God the Son, you lived a life of love, died on the Cross, and rose from the dead, you gave us the gift of the Holy Spirit.
We worship and adore you.
God the Holy Spirit, you come into our lives, to help us and give us guidance, you call us to a life of faith and service.
We worship and adore you.
Triune God - One in Three and Three in One,
We worship and adore you.   **Amen**
(Based on Companion to Lectionary - Trinity Sunday)
© Copyright - Epworth Press; used by kind permission

"BOIL IN THE BAG" MEDITATION 42

Many years ago the ruler of a Chinese province met some people from England and was highly impressed by the British character. He asked how such a character had been acquired, and was informed that one of the contributing factors was participation in games and sports, especially team games, and in particular football. The ruler decided that his people must learn to play football and immediately arranged for a copy of the rules to be made available. The rules were translated into Chinese and hundreds of copies distributed to all the schools in that province and the children made to learn the rules by heart. "Now", said the ruler, "everyone can play football." How wrong can you be, for not one of them had ever had any practice.

As an NCO in The Boys' Brigade, in order to gain my Proficiency Badge I had to sit a three hour written examination paper, all the questions being based on a knowledge of The Boys' Handbook and The Boys' Brigade Drill Book. Such an award no longer exists but in those days it was not enough for an NCO to know how to drill but he had to know how to teach it as well. Even now, some forty six years later, I can remember the sequence of instruction for any particular movement. It was:

explanation - demonstration - execution - repetition.

This sequence is very useful in teaching a very wide range of subjects and its application is common sense. For example, how did you learn to master some of the basic techniques of mathematics - the multiplying or dividing of fractions - the solving of simple equations - were you able to do them by just having someone explaining what to do, the explanation being in words alone? Of course not, that explanation had to be accompanied by a practical demonstration, using the blackboard, the overhead projector or some other form of visual aid. Just telling the pupils was not enough, it had to be followed by a demonstration and application. The same thing is even more true when it comes to practical subjects - try explaining how to make a coil pot (without using your hands) - or how to prepare and cook a 'toad in the hole', without reference to an illustration or diagram. Once again some form of demonstration is essential if we are to meet with any success in doing a thing ourselves - we learn by following the example of others. But, listening and watching are still not enough if we are to master a procedure or skill for ourselves - that only comes with repetition - repeated practice, doing it over and over again. As the proverb puts it - 'practice makes perfect'.

There is a sense in which this idea is repeating the contents of the previous 'menu' in a different way - The Trinity consists of God the Father, God the Son and God the Holy Spirit - through the old testament writings and prophets God the Father explained his ideas on how men could live together in peace and understanding - but that explanation was insufficient, it needed a demonstration that could be seen in real life so he sent his Son to show us how - but to know how is one thing, to be able to do it is another. That's where the Holy Spirit comes in - he gives us the guidance, help and encouragement we need to do it for ourselves - he is the 'enabler'. Then, in time, practice and perfection become second nature.

Menu Master 43

On being a critic - 1

A schoolboy's dilemma

Reading - St Matthew 7 v 1 - 5

"Do not judge others, so that God will not judge you, for God will judge you in the same way as you judge others, and he will apply to you the rules you apply to others. Why then do you look for a speck of dust in your brother's eye, and pay no attention to the log in your own?"

Hymns & Psalms 739

May the mind of Christ my Saviour
Live in me from day to day,
By his love and power controlling,
All I do and say.

May the word of God dwell richly
In my heart from hour to hour
So that all may see I triumph
Only through his power
Kate Barclay Wilkinson (1859-1928)

Prayer:

Father God, we need your help,
Not so much to know what is right - we know that already;
but help to do what is right:
We need help to resist temptations which come from inside ourselves
as well as the persuasions of others
Help us never to be afraid to do the right thing:
to be what you want us to be and to do what you want us to do.

Amen

"BOIL IN THE BAG" MEDITATION 43

A Schoolboy's Dilemma

When I take a long time . . . . I am being slow.
When my teacher takes a long time . . . he is being thorough.
When I fail to do something . . . . I am being lazy.
When my teacher doesn't do it . . . . he's far too busy.
When I do something without being told . . . I'm being smart.
When he does the same . . . . that's using his initiative.
When I try to please the teacher . . . . I'm a creep.
When he pleases the headmaster . . . . . . that's co-operation.
When I do something right . . . . the teacher never remembers.
When I do something wrong . . . . he never forgets.

When I think of that quotation - which I 'cribbed' from someone else's assembly - I remind myself that on many similar times I have quickly taken out my diary and written notes that I can use on a future occasion. I wonder what others think when they see me writing instead of listening? How would I react if a pupil did the same thing? I am sure I would jump to the wrong conclusion and say something like, "Doing your homework? Why not finish it before you come to school?" Is this not another aspect of prejudice - to prejudge the circumstances without knowing all the facts?

So many people, and they don't have to be teachers, are quite prepared to criticise, or even condemn, the actions of others and at the same time justify themselves for doing exactly the same thing. How did Jesus put it? Why do you look for a speck of dust in someone's eye, when you can hardly see what you are doing for the plank of wood that is sticking out from your own. We tend to jump to conclusions without considering the facts.

I will always remember being in the middle of a maths lesson when the PE master came into my classroom and asked if Chris was in school that day. Chris was a keen athletic type and represented his school in a number of sporting activities. Recently, however, there had been a tendency for him to be absent on the days he was required and one jumped to the conclusion he was 'bunking' when he didn't feel like playing. The PE master more or less said so as he left the room. As soon as he had gone, Doug, one of Chris's friends, in fact his next door neighbour, informed me that he didn't think Chris was 'bunking' on this occasion because the doctor had called at the house about five o'clock that morning. I immediately sent Doug to clarify the situation with the PE staff. It was a good job I did for within the hour the secretary called me from my classroom and informed me that Chris's father had just telephoned to say his son had died in hospital that morning. Apparently he had developed diabetes and the parents hadn't recognised it.

Before you criticise or offer an opinion make sure you know the facts. The Indians have a proverb - 'No man has the right to find fault with another until he has walked a mile in his moccasins'. I suppose that is the same as our saying 'put yourself in his shoes'. Try to understand his circumstances and the conditions he has to face in life. What are his needs?

Menu Master 44

On being a critic - 2

Out of retirement

Reading - Romans 2 v 1 - 8

Do not, my friend, pass judgement on others. You have no excuse at all, whoever you are. For when you judge others and then do the same things which they do, you condemn yourself. We know that God is right when he judges the people who do such things as these. But you, my friend, do those very things for which you pass judgement on others.

Hymns & Psalms 748

Teach me, O Lord, thy holy way,
And give me an obedient mind,
That in thy service I may find
My soul's delight from day to day.

Guide me, O Saviour, with thy hand,
And so control my thoughts and deeds,
That I may tread the path which leads
Right onward to the blessed land.
William Tidd Matson (1833-99)

Prayer:

Father God,
Help us not to think of how much we can get out of life,
but of how much we can put into it.
Help us not to conentrate on getting; but on how much we can give.
Not on using people; but on being useful to them.
We ask this, so that your kingdom of love may grow.   Amen

"BOIL IN A BAG" MEDITATION 44

Having retired after over forty years in the teaching profession, I felt I still had something to contribute and decided to try my hand at 'supply work', the condition being that I would teach mathematics, after all I had been teaching that subject for so long I felt it could present very few problems. That is what I thought but when it came 'to the crunch' things did not work out like that at all. I soon found a suitable school - unfortunately a newly appointed teacher had met with an accident during the summer holidays and although she had taken up the appointment, she found the injury she had suffered to her leg was more complicated than had at first been diagnosed. With the result she was advised to take at least six weeks off to let the injury heal. So, her timetable now became mine. It seemed quite straight forward - very similar in many ways to what I had been used to.

There was one big difference however, I had been used to my own room with all the lessons taught in one place - my own little kingdom - I knew where everything was and I arranged the desks in the way I wanted them - an arrangement suited to my style of discipline. I now found my lessons were to be taken in different rooms and my books had to be transported wherever I went. To make matters worse some rooms had the desks in blocks, some side by side across the room, few seemed to arrange them in the familiar columns I preferred. I soon realised also, when opting for this new style of life, I had failed to take into consideration one of the basic facts for good discipline - children do not like constant changes of staff - they prefer the security of continuity - this, to them, is more important than the standard of teaching. After twenty five years in one school I had forgotten what it was like to have to establish myself all over again. Previously my reputation was known to the pupils - even before they came to the school for the first time - since in many cases I had taught not only their older brothers and sisters I had even taught their parents as well.

At the end of that first day as I travelled home on the M25 - another new experience, for I had been used to the slower, and less hazardous A13, I wondered if I had done the right thing after all - this was the time of life when I should be relaxing, not looking for a new, exhausting and taxing experience. As things worked out I stayed at the school for almost a term and by the end of that time I had been accepted by the children and had a good working relationship with them, but this did not alter my feelings and remembrance of that first day. Strangely enough the experience did me a lot of good - it made me think again about the situation all new members of staff, even experienced teachers, find themselves in. I had had it all too easy for too long and I had forgotten what it was like to face some of the difficult circumstances others so often find themselves in. In fact, when a senior member of staff asked me how things were going, I told him it would be a good idea if those, in a similar position to himself, spent a few days in another school every now and again so that they could appreciate the problems of others, and so be more supportive and sympathetic. That is a lesson we might all do well to learn. Do not be critical of others unless you can imagine yourself in their position first.

Menu Master 45

Thomas

Yours undoubtedly

Reading - St John 20 v 24 - 29

One of the twelve disciples, Thomas, was not with them when Jesus came. So the other disciples told him, "We have seen the Lord!" Thomas said to them, "Unless I see the scars of the nails in his hands, and put my fingers in those scars and my hand in his side, I will not believe." A week later the disciples were together again and Thomas was with them. Jesus came and said to them, "Peace be with you." Then he said to Thomas, "Put your finger here and look at my hands. Stop your doubting and believe." Thomas answered him, "My Lord and my God."

Hymns & Psalms 212

> No more we doubt thee, glorious Prince of Life,
> Life is nought without thee; aid us in our strife;
> Make us more than conquerors through thy deathless love
> Bring us safe through Jordan to thy home above.
> > Thine be the glory, risen, conquering Son;
> > Endless in the victory thou o'er death hast won.
> > > *Edmond L. Budry (1854-1932)*
> > > *tr. Richard B. Hoyle (1875-1939)*

Prayer: Gracious God, in the journey of life, you are before us leading us on and preparing a way that opens up new horizons which bring challenge and purpose.
Gracious God, in the journey of life, you are beside us, guide and helper, companion of the way, showing us so many opportunities.
Gracious God, in the journey of life, you are within us, making our thoughts and actions, the way of your saving love in our world, giving service and inspiration through us.
Gracious God, we give you the praise.   Amen

"BOIL IN THE BAG" MEDITATION 45

Understandably the story of the resurrection is told by each of the Gospel writers - again, understandably, each writer recalls the incident as he saw it or how it had been described to him. Four writers - four versions - and the most popular seems to be the one in the Gospel of St John. I wonder why? Is it because John mentions Thomas, the only one to do so, and Thomas doubted what he had been told. Doubting Thomas, the story portraits him as being rather weak and negative. Poor old Thomas - history seems to have forgotten everything else he did and remembers him for one thing - he doubted. Did you realise also that John is the only one who tells us anything else about Thomas - the other gospels only include his name in the lists of disciples - no more than that. Nothing to tell us what kind of man he really was - no reference to his supreme loyalty - no mention of his supreme bravery - John alone tells us of both of these qualities and yet - our memories are such that these outstanding, positive qualities are both hidden by the fact that he has gone through history as the supreme pessimist.

I wonder where Thomas was when Jesus first appeared? Grief can be a strange thing - and we react in different ways. Some look for the companionship of friends and relatives, others want to be on their own coming to terms with the situation in their own way. Thomas, I feel was like that - a very deep thinker, he had shown this same quality a short time before when Jesus told his disciples he was going to die and then added, "you know where I am going and you know the way." It was Thomas who then spoke up, "Lord, we don't know where you are going, so how can we know the way?" He didn't just accept things for their face value, he had to think them through for himself. He was completely honest and would not say he was sure of anything of which he was not sure, and he would not say he believed anything that he did not believe. Is that wrong?

Let us look at another story - Jesus had received news that his friend Lazarus was very ill - then the sadder news: Lazarus had died. Lazarus and his sisters lived at Bethany, a village not far from Jerusalem, so close in fact, Jesus spent a couple of nights there during that last eventful week before Good Friday. At the time of Lazarus' death it was also very apparent that the leaders in Jerusalem were determined to kill Jesus and everyone knew it - so when Jesus suggested he was going to Bethany to visit the family, it was like walking into the lions' den - it was inviting certain death and the disciples were very reluctant to go with him. It was at this time that Thomas spoke up - "Let us also go that we may die with him." What kind of man is that? A weakling? He rallied the others - that statement showed great loyalty, it also showed great courage. Real courage. It is not being courageous to do something when we have no fear - it is knowing what the consequences might be and still going ahead. There is a great deal more to Thomas than most people realise. That is true of all people, the trouble is we just remember the wrong bits - we tend to remember bad things and forget the good.

Which brings us back to the saying - 'When I do something right, no one remembers - when I do something wrong, no one forgets.'

Menu Master 46

Barnabas

Taking second place

Reading - Acts 4 v 32 - 36

The group of believers was one in mind and heart. No one said that any of his belongings was his own, but they all shared with one another everything they had. With great power the apostles gave witness to the resurrection of the Lord Jesus, and God poured out rich blessings on them all. And so it was that Joseph, a Levite born in Cyprus, whom the apostles called Barnabas (which means 'One who Encourages') sold a field he owned, brought the money and handed it over to the apostles.

Hymns & Psalms 553 (verses 1 & 6)

> Lord speak to me, that I may speak
>   In living echoes of thy tone;
>   As thou hast sought, so let me seek
>   Thy erring children lost and lone.
>
> O use me, Lord, use even me,
>   Just as thou wilt, and when, and where,
>   Until thy blessed face I see,
>   Thy rest, thy joy, thy glory share.
>   *Frances Ridley Havergal (1836-79)*

Prayer: Father, in all our friendships, may we be faithful people whose actions are generous and whose word can be trusted. Help us to listen in true conversation to the people with whom we live or work in a way that builds up friendship. May we learn to put honesty before popularity, and be ready to change our minds when we have grown to understand people better. Always ready to give in friendship may we also be ready to receive so that friendship grows on both sides.

In the name of him who called us his friends.   Amen

"BOIL IN THE BAG" MEDITATION 46

During the First World War a white feather became the symbol of cowardice and people used to give them to the civilians they thought should be in the armed forces. Collie Knox was a member of The Royal Flying Corps - the equivalent of the RAF today - during the war he had been badly smashed up in a flying acccident. On the day in question he was dining out with a friend in London, neither of them in uniform, and half way through the meal a girl came up and handed to each a white feather. She thought the worst but she was very mistaken for that very morning his friend had been to Buckingham Palace where he was decorated for his bravery. How wrong we can be at times in criticising others without knowing all the facts.

Think for a moment of one of the lesser known characters in the New Testament - a man called Barnabas - although that was only a nickname - his real name was Joseph. In those days Barnabas meant one who was kind and caring, one who concerned about the needs of others, doing all he could to help them. How would you like a nickname like that - or would it make you feel a bit of a wimp? Barnabas was far from that, as a Levite. It was the priests who occupied the limelight - they carried out the great sacrifices which everyone could see and admire. It was the duty of a Levite to sweep the floor or open a door - the menial, the servant type jobs. The main sacrifice Barnabas had made was his wealth; he sacrificed that so that he could help others. Barnabas is frequently associated with Saul (later called Paul). When Saul suddenly became a Christian, many people did not believe him or trust him. In their opinion he was just a confidence trickster trying to get inside information but Barnabas was prepared to believe him and accepted his story. While others looked for the worst, he looked only for the best, just as Jesus had done with Peter and Matthew.

As time went on, Barnabas and Saul became great friends and worked closely together, first in Antioch then they went on to Cyprus - it was at Paphos on the island of Cyprus that Saul is first referred to as Paul but it is also worth noting that as their story unfolds we no longer read about Barnabas and Saul but Paul and Barnabas - it wasn't only a change of name, but one of status too, Paul had become the leader and Barnabas had to take second place - but he was prepared to do so.

That attitude in life is not always easy. We tend to try and better ourselves rather than 'take a back seat', we hate to be passed over - ambition makes us look for promotion, which can be a good thing - but we must also take into consideration the feelings of others. Man can be very selfish, he hates to be hurt, but he doesn't mind hurting the feelings of others. You will find that at school, at work, and even in the church, there are those who cling to their position long after they have ceased to be useful, even if another has been chosen who can do the work more effectively. They are not prepared to see someone else occupy the place they once held. They feel no one can do the job better than they can. Barnabas could occupy the first or the second place equally willingly, all that mattered was that the work must go on, and he was even prepared to help the one who was chosen to replace him.

Menu Master 47

John Mark - 1

Through the keyhole

Reading - Acts 12 v 6 - 16

Peter was sleeping between two guards. He was tied with chains and guards were on duty. Suddenly an angel of the Lord stood there, shook Peter by the shoulder, woke him and said, "Hurry! Get up!" At once the chains fell off Peter's hands. They passed by the first guard post and then the second and came at last to the iron gate leading into the city. The gate opened for them by itself - then the angel left him. Aware of his situation, he went to the home of Mary, the mother of John Mark where many people had gathered and were praying.

Hymns & Psalms 594

An Upper Room did our Lord prepare
For those he loved until the end;
And his disciples still gather there
To celebrate their Risen Friend.
And after supper he washed their feet
For service too, is sacrament;
In him our joy shall be complete -
Sent out to serve, as he was sent.
F. Pratt Green (1903-)
© *Copyright, Stainer & Bell Ltd., used by permission.*

A Prayer (H&P 597) James Montgomery:
Be known to us in breaking bread
But do not then depart;
Saviour, abide with us, and spread
Thy table in our heart.
Amen

Ingredients enclosed

serve to taste

'Through the keyhole' is a television programme in which the audience is taken on a guided tour of the home of a well known personality. The tour always finishes with the question 'who lives in a house like this?' A celebrity panel then question the presenter in an attempt to find out whose home it is. Perhaps one day someone will come up with a variation on this programme, showing houses of historical significance, for example, the house Jesus used so often towards the end of his life. The disciples continued to meet there even after the resurrection of Christ: perhaps people have come to think of it, not so much as a house, but a room - The Upper Room - but someone must have lived in the rest of the house. So who lived in a house like that?

Over the years, that upper room, the room where Jesus was joined by his disciples for the last supper, has become a favourite subject for many an artist, perhaps the most famous being the wall painting by Leonardo da Vinci in Milan - completed in 1482. There is a legend attributed to that painting. It tells how da Vinci used various people to portray the characters he wished to create. Starting with Jesus, he walked the streets until he found the right person for each character. Eventually the painting was almost complete, just one more person remained, that was Judas - where could he find someone with a face that showed such bitterness and hatred, one who was ready to betray his closest friend? When he found him, he invited him to his studio only to find the man broke down and cried as he said, "When you first started this painting you chose me as Jesus! How could I have changed that much?"

The upper room is mentioned in each of the four gospels but not one of them tell us who owned the house - the only clue comes in the writings of Mark - like the others he tells how Jesus left the house and went to the Garden of Gethsemane where he was arrested. The disciples left him and ran away, but Mark tells of a young man 'who was dressed only in a linen cloth' - they tried to arrest him too, but he dropped the linen cloth and fled naked - the streaker of Gethsemane. The only reason Mark knew of such an incident was because he was that young man - his was the home into which Jesus went. When Jesus left, although he was in bed, Mark was curious to know what was happening so he grabbed the sheet that covered him and followed.

This evidence is later confirmed by the writer of The Acts of the Apostles who tells how, after his release from prison, Peter went back to the same house, and he refers to it as the home of Mary, the mother of John Mark. In those days the Romans were masters of Palestine, so all Jews had two names, John was his Jewish name, the name used by his family and close friends and Mark (or Marcus) was his Roman name, the name by which he was known to anyone else. This young man had a very good start in life, he came from a good home with a very caring mother. His parents were considerate and generous. He also had a wealthy and influential uncle who did a great deal to help him - but John Mark had to learn to stand on his own two feet and not rely on the efforts of others - and, as we will see in a later menu, that is where he almost came unstuck.

Menu Master 48

The Call of God

Boys will be ...?

Reading - 1 Samuel 3 v 1 - 10

One night Eli, who was almost blind, was sleeping in his own room; Samuel was sleeping in the sanctuary, where the sacred Covenant Box was. Before dawn, while the lamp was still burning, the Lord called Samuel. He answered, "Yes, sir!" and ran to Eli and said, "You called me, and here I am." But Eli answered, "I didn't call you, go back to bed." This happened three times, so the third time Eli, realising it was the Lord who was calling, said to Samuel, "If he calls you again, say, 'Speak Lord, for your servant is listening.'"

Hymns & Psalms 523

O give me Samuel's ear, the open ear, O Lord,
Alive and quick to hear each whisper of thy word.
Like him to answer at thy call,
And to obey thee first of all.

O give me Samuel's heart, a lowly heart that waits
Where in thy house thou art, or watches at thy gates;
By day or night - a heart that still
Moves at the breathing of thy will.
James Drummond Burns (1823-64)

Prayer: Together we have listened to the stories of those you have called to follow and serve you, now as individuals let each of us pray, that you
will
Open my eyes that I may see
The work that you have set for me;
And help me daily by your grace
Your will to do, your steps to trace.
Amen

"BOIL IN THE BAG" MEDITATION 48

I joined the Grays Methodist Sunday School when I was twelve years old. Every year one weekend was given over to special Anniversary Services and a part of this was normally a 'Demonstration' by the pupils. It took various forms and included music and drama. One of the first I took part in was called 'Advertisements' - some formed a choir and others were chosen to recite a short poem suitable for the specially printed advertisements which were carried on large boards. I had a speaking part, mainly because I couldn't sing. My advert was 'Boy Wanted'. I was very nervous, and frightened I would forget the words, so I wrote them on a piece of paper and stuck them to the back of the board. I didn't need the paper, and can still remember the words fifty years later. Little did I realise at the time, how, as I grew older that simple poem would be the pattern of my life.

> Boy wanted! 'Tis a notice clear,and it appeals to me,
> Henceforth I have determined Lord they humble son to be
> And if I wander from the way, if I grow weak or slack,
> Send out thy clarion call of love and bring me swiftly back.

'Boys will be Boys' is not only a somewhat hackneyed expression, it is also chronologically inaccurate. The Rev George Potter wrote a poem that begins - 'He's only a boy but he's the man of tomorrow this boy of today.' So let us consider the thought 'Boys will be Men'. I have often wondered when I look at the pupils in my class, what they will make of life. Or perhaps more correctly, what life will make for them. The bible is full of stories of boys who started out in life in one direction and then found themselves going in a completely different way. Think of the boy who strutted around in a coat of many colours - the very sight of that coat brought hatred, bitterness and violence to the minds of his brothers - but God had others plans. Joseph was a boy born to guide, to help and to serve his people.

Then there was another, in outward appearance an Egyptian but in fact he was an Israelite who was forced to watch his own people as they struggled in slavery. Years before, his mother had made plans for him, but so had God - Moses was chosen to lead his people to the promised land. In the New Testament it is the same - can't you imagine two young lads helping their father as they repair the nets ready for a fishing trip. Like father, like son - surely they would carry on the family business one day - but God needed them for His work and so Jesus said to Andrew and Peter, "Follow me, and I will make you fishers of men."

As history unfolds we cannot count the number to whom God has spoken. In 1883 William Alexander Smith, founded The Boys' Brigade - its Object, 'The advancement of Christ's Kingdom among Boys' and I have often wondered if part of the inspiration behind his work was the story of the feeding of the 5000 - William Smith was born in Scotland and Andrew is Scotland's Patron Saint - in the story, Andrew found the boy with the food and said, "Lord, there is a lad here." Through the influence of William Smith many boys have been introduced to Jesus, and as a result their lives have been completely changed.

Menu Master 49

John Mark - 2

A Second Chance

Reading - Acts 15 v 36 - 41

Some time later Paul said to Barnabas, "Let us go back and visit our brothers in every town where we have preached the word of the Lord, and let us find out how they are getting on." Barnabas wanted to take John Mark with them, but Paul did not think it was right to take him, because he had not stayed with them to the end of their earlier mission, but had turned back at Pamphylia.   There was a sharp argument, and they separated: Barnabas took Mark and sailed off for Cyprus, while Paul chose Silas and went through Syria and Cilicia strengthening the churches.

Rejoice and Sing 575

God of mercy, God of grace,
   Show the brightness of thy face;
Shine upon us Saviour shine,
   Fill your Church with light divine,
And your saving health extend,
   Unto earth's remotest end.
Henry Francis Lyte (1793-1847)

Prayer: Father, only you know how much we need forgiveness, and only you can forgive.
Grant us freedom from the past,
resolve in the present,
and dedication in the future,
that we may be better disciples of Jesus Christ
your Son. For his sake.   Amen

"BOIL IN THE BAG" MEDITATION 49

Let us bring together two previous 'menus' - those of Barnabas and John Mark - Barnabas was the influential uncle of John Mark and he took John Mark with him when he went on a missionary journey with Paul - this was the time when Paul took over the leadership. They had travelled from Antioch to Cyprus and then on to Asia Minor. Paul was quite happy about the arrangement of taking the younger man along. At first everything went well, Barnabas had been born in Cyprus so it was very possible John Mark was on familiar territory when they visited that island, but from there they sailed to the mainland, going to Perga and planned to make an expedition inland travelling to the central plateau. It was at this point that John Mark had had enough, he quit and returned home. Several reasons have been put forward for this, he was young and inexperienced, he may have been frightened as to what was ahead of him, or he may simply have become homesick, in any case he went back to Jerusalem and left the others, who went on and finished their intended journey.

Some time later this incident was remembered by Paul and when he made it know that he was going back to see how the various groups of Christians were getting on, he invited Barnabas to go with him. Barnabas accepted the invitation and suggested John Mark should go as well. This led to quite a disagreement between them - Paul pointing out that John Mark had let them down once and he was not prepared to give him a second chance. The quarrel was so fierce that they parted company. Paul took another man named Silas and the two set off for Syria - leaving Barnabas and John Mark to return, yet again, to Cyprus.

This attitude of Paul's has always concerned me, I thought he would have given him that second chance - just as Barnabas had. Barnabas found it in his heart to forgive - just as Jesus would have done. So many relationships are spoilt, so many opportunities lost, because people bear a grudge and are not prepared to give others the benefit of the doubt. Fortunately Paul did change his attitude later in life and a great friendship grew up between the two of them.

I will always remember a young lad named Lee, who was due to transfer to our secondary school in the September. I had previously visited his class in the nearby primary school and explained something of the procedure involved and the opportunities they would get. Fortunately the two schools were quite close together so I had also told them that if anything worried them and they wanted to chat about it they could come over and see me and we could discuss the matter that was causing concern. Lee accepted the invitation. He told me he had a very bad record in his primary school and was always getting into trouble. He wanted to know if this would go against him when he 'came up', as he put it. Another expression he used was, 'Will the slate be wiped clean?' He obviously wanted a chance to start again. I told him I appreciated his honesty and said it was very apparent, since he was so concerned, that he intended to try and do better and the 'slate would be wiped clean'.

Mind you it didn't take him long to fill it up again.

Menu Master 50

Sincerity

Without wax

Reading - 1 Corinthians 13 v 1 - 13

Love is patient and kind: it is not jealous, conceited or proud: love is not ill-mannered or selfish or irritable: love does not keep a record of wrongs: love is not happy with evil, but is happy with the truth. Love never gives up: and its faith, hope and patience never fail. When I was a child, my speech, feelings and thinking were those of a child: now that I am a man, I have no use for childish ways. Meanwhile these three remain; faith, hope and love: and the greatest of these is love.

Hymns & Psalms 742

O Jesus Christ, grow thou in me.
  And all things else recede;
My heart be daily nearer thee,
  From sin be daily freed.

Make this poor self grow less and less,
  Be thou my life and aim;
O make me daily, through thy grace,
  More meet to bear thy name.
Johann Casper Lavater (1741-1801)
tr Elizabeth Lee Smith (1817-98)

A Prayer of Dean Vaughan

O Lord God, give us grace to set a good example to all amongst whom we live, to be just and true in all our dealings, to be strict and conscientious in the discharge of every duty, kind and charitable and courteous towards all men: so that the mind of Jesus Christ may be formed in us, and all men take knowledge of us that we are his disciples. Through Christ our Lord, Amen

"BOIL IN THE BAG MEDITATION 50

During the half term holiday two boys decided they would go into the city to have a look round. After visiting a number of large shops they ventured into an art gallery. Their teacher had told them about this particular gallery during one of their lessons. She had told them that if they had the opportunity they should not miss seeing the wonderful collection of marble statues there. They took her advice and soon found the room she had mentioned. Their appreciation of how such works of art had been made, differed considerably. The first boy said how difficult it must be, and how long it must have taken to create such beautiful things. The second one disagreed, for, as he put it, 'all you have to do is take a large chunk of marble and knock off the bits you don't want.'

Whenever I think of that particular story I wonder what would happen if, in making such a statue, you 'knocked off' the wrong bit by mistake. A popular television advert found one possible solution - the sculptor simply struck a match and lit a Hamlet cigar, that solved all his problems, but it is no solution in real life. Many a sculptor corrected small errors by using a special wax, one which could only be detected by an expert. The perfect statue was one created without wax. The Latin word for 'wax' is 'cera' and that for 'without' is 'sine' - if a statue was to be perfect it was to be 'sine-cera' or sincere. Sincere means being genuine not false, living without fault. We often finish a letter, 'Yours sincerely', are we really being completely honest in using such a phrase?

Are we genuine in our attitude to others - our family and our friends? Are we always honest with ourselves - or do we live in 'cloud cuckoo land'? There is only one man who could claim his life had been without fault - his attitude to others was the perfect example - that was Jesus. He looked only for the best in others, he was prepared to forgive others when things went wrong. Peter once asked him how many times he should forgive someone and suggested seven times might be the limit - "No, not seven times," said Jesus, "but seventy times seven." He then went on to tell a story of how a king decided to check his accounts and soon discovered one of his servants had been 'fiddling the books' and a very large sum of money was missing. In consequence he told the man he was to be sold as a slave, together with his wife and children and all he possessed, in order to pay the debt. The servant pleaded for mercy - the king felt sorry for him - forgave him the debt and let him go. Then what did this man do? He immediately found someone else who owed him only a few pounds - and had him imprisoned for such a petty crime! It is so easy for those, who expect God to be so patient, and to understand their weaknesses and shortcomings, to bear a grudge against someone else over some insignificant act or thoughtless comment.

When Paul wrote a letter to the Philippians he said, 'Let this mind be in you which was also in Christ Jesus' - in other words aim only for the best and don't let your standards drop. Let your life be genuine - without fault - sincere in your attitude to others and with yourself.

USEFUL NOTES FOR PREPARATION

No two people will present any given 'menu' in the same way, but I strongly recommend extra preparation by using visual-aids with certain of them.

Menu 1
The use of a large sheet of paper with the figures already written out and a couple of calculators available to allow a check on your calculations. Active participation, if only by a couple of those present, helps to keep the interest of the others.

Menu 8
Have the word GH O TI prepared in such a way that it can be broken down and then reassembled.

Menu 11
Try to get hold of a Poppy Wreath - preferably one that will be placed at the cenotraph locally - also you may wish to sell poppies after the talk.

Menu 19
Flash cards will come in handy here - with the numbers 366 - 122 - 70 - 18 - etc. clearly displayed.

Menu 26
Why not have the appropriate music playing before you start - some may know the music, but not by name.

Menu 27
Further information of Tear Fund and 'Compassion has heart' (Cliff's latest video for Tear Fund) - Contact: Tear Fund Resources, 100 Church Road, Teddington, Middlesex TW11 8QE Tel: 081 977 9144

Menu 38
Have a black board and easel available to help with your 'sums'.

Menu 39
Before you use this 'menu' I suggest you place various sizes of large footprint cut-outs on two side walls. On each cut-out will be a number, 4, 14, 24 ... up to 74. Make no reference to these until you get to the point about various ages - 'put yourself in someone else's shoes.'. The visual helps the impact of the spoken word.

AN ALTERNATIVE "BOIL IN THE BAG" MEDITATION FOR EASTER

Paul Robeson, the great singer of negro spiritual songs, gave his first concert in this country at The Dome in Brighton. He was an instant success, so much so that the audience called for encore after encore, and each was greeted with a standing ovation. Paul Robeson wondered if he would ever be able to leave the platform. Eventually he had a word with his pianist and then started to sing again - this time there was no applause, no standing ovation - the audience simply sat in silence. As he left the platform he said to someone nearby, "That was the loudest applause of all." Why the change? He had just sung - 'Were you there when they crucified my Lord?"

Congregation sing verse 1 of Hymns & Psalms 181
> Were you there when they crucified my Lord?
> Were you there when they crucified my Lord?
> Oh! Sometimes in causes me to tremble, tremble, tremble.
> Were you there when they crucified my Lord?

When midnight came, Jesus rose from the table in the upper room and led His disciples out to Gethsemane. He went forward to pray alone in the dark. He lay with His face to the ground, and the agony none may ever comprehend began. "O my Father, if it be possible let this cup pass from me." It was not death that made him cry to God - it was sin. It was the burden of all the sins of men, the shame of all the world, which in that dread hour He was taking upon His own sinless heart. We can only stand afar off and hear the cry out of the darkness, "O God let this cup pass," but then we hear another cry - a prayer calm and resolute - "If this cup may not pass from me, except I drink it, Thy will be done."

Congregation sing verse 2
> Were you there when they nailed Him to the Cross?

It was towards evening when Joseph of Arimathea arrived, he went boldly into the presence of Pilate and asked for the body of Jesus. Pilate was surprised to hear that Jesus was already dead and called for a report. Having heard the report permission was granted and Joseph took the body down, wrapped it in a linen sheet and placed it in a tomb which had been dug out of solid rock. He then rolled a large stone across the entrance to the tomb. (Mark 15 v 42 - 47)

Congregation sing verse 3
> Were you there when they laid Him in the tomb?

In 'The Trial Of Jesus' there is a striking passage in which Longinus, the Roman centurion in command of the soldiers at the Cross, comes back to Pilate and hands in his report on the day's work. The report is given, when Procula, Pilate's wife asks "Do you think He is dead?" "No lady," he replies, "I don't." "Then where is He?" "Let loose in the world lady, where neither Roman nor Jew can stop His truth."

Conclude as congregation sing verse 4
> Were you there when God raised Him from the tomb?
>> Were you there when God raised Him from the tomb?
>> Oh! Sometimes it causes me to tremble, tremble, tremble.
>> Were you there when God raised Him from the tomb?

Menu Master

Peace

The first 'battle'

Reading - Genesis 4 v 2 - 9

Abel became a shepherd but Cain was a farmer. After some time Cain brought some of his harvest and gave it as an offering to the Lord. Then Abel brought the first born lamb to one of his sheep, killed it, and gave the best parts of it as an offering. The Lord was pleased with Abel and his offering, but he rejected Cain and his offering. The Lord said to Cain, "Why are you angry? Why that scowl on your face? If you had done the right thing you would be smiling." Then Cain said to Abel, "Let's go out in the fields." When they were out in the fields, Cain turned on his brother and killed him.

Hymns & Psalms 776 (verse2)

> Make me a channel of your peace
> Where there's despair in life, let me bring hope;
> Where there is darkness, only light,
> And where there's sadness, ever joy:
>
> O, Master grant that I may never seek
> So much to be consoled as to console;
> To be understood as to understand;
> To be loved, as to love with all my soul.

Prayer: Lord, make us forgiving to each other, gentle and generous to everybody else we meet, following the example of Christ himself, who in the face of hatred persisted in love, opening the way for all mankind, from despair to hope, from death to life. Amen

"BOIL IN THE BAG" MEDITATION
An alternative study for the meaning of 'Peace'

One of the earliest stories in the bible is to be found in the fourth chapter of the Book of Genesis, it tells how Cain and Abel, the sons of Adam and Eve, had a dispute that ended in murder. Abel had become a shepherd, Cain a farmer - after some time both made an offering to God - the first Harvest Festival, if you like. The difference in their gifts was quite simply that whereas Abel gave the best of his flock, Cain just gave 'something', any old thing would do. The Lord praised Abel but criticized Cain with the result that Cain waited for his opportunity and killed his brother. When the Lord approached Cain and asked where Abel was, Cain's immediate response was, 'Am I my brother's keeper, am I supposed to take care of him?'

St John, who wrote his gospel to tell us something of the inner life of Jesus also wrote an epistle (there are three under the name of John) I am referring to the first and in this he talks about the inner life of the Christian. Chapter 3, verse 11 says:

> "The message you heard from the very beginning is this: we must love one another. We must not be like Cain, he belonged to the Evil One and murdered his own brother Abel. Why did Cain murder Abel? Because the things he himself did were wrong, but the things his brother did were right. So do not be surprised, my brothers, if the people of the world hate you. Whoever hates his brother is a murderer, and you know that a murderer has not got eternal life in him. (NB v 16 cf John 3 v 16) This is how we know what love is: Christ gave his life for us. We too ought to give our lives for our brothers! If a rich person sees his brother in need, yet closes his heart against him, how can he claim he loves God? My children, our love must not be just words and talk, it must be true love, which shows itself in action."

Genesis 4 tells us that:
> Peace involves looking at the causes of conflict - Peace involves mutual responsibility.

1 John 3 tells us that:
> Peace involves Love to the point of sacrifice - Peace must be practical.

Now let us turn to the Gospel of St John and see what Jesus had to say about peace - we find his words in chapter fourteen - Jesus is talking about our love for him and how we react to his commandments he has given and then in verse 25 goes on to say: "I have told you this while I am still with you. The Helper, the Holy Spirit, whom the Father will send in my name, will teach you everything and may you remember all that I have told you. Peace is what I leave with you; it is my own peace that I give you. I do not give it as the world does. Do not be worried and upset; do not be afraid."

St John 14 tells us that: Peace is to be found through our relationship with God.

All 3 passages tell us: Peace involves not only goodwill, but struggle and conflict.

A "BOIL IN THE BAG" MEDITATION
A Reading - A Hymn - A Prayer - An Expressed Thought

"BOIL IN THE BAG" DAY MEDITATION FOR MOTHER'S DAY

A Mother is a Beacon

A mother is a beacon
Who shines out bright and clear
Reminding all her children
That help is always near.

A Mother is a lighthouse
Which shows the safest ways
To avoid life's sharpest rocks
A Mother's Love

A mother, like a tugboat,
Will strain with all her might
To bring her children safely
To havens calm and bright.

A mother is a harbour
Where weary young ones rest
Then set out with strength renewed
Their own ideas to test.

A mother is a coastcard
Who acts when danger's near
Persuading these her loved ones
A better course to steer.

Kathleen M. Clark
© Moorley's Ilkeston from 'A Celebration of Mothers'
- A Resource Book for Mothering Sunday

A Prayer of Thanksgiving
(from Hymns & Psalms - 572 verses 4 & 6)

Think of a world without any poetry,
  Think of a book without any words.
Think of a song without any music,
  Think of a hymn without any words.
We thank you Lord, for poetry and music,
We thank you, Lord, and praise your holy name.

Think of the world without any people,
  Think of a street with no one living there,
Think of a town without any houses,
  No one to love and nobody to care:
We thank you, Lord, for families and friendships,
We thank you, Lord, and praise your holy name.
Doreen Newport
© *Copyright, Stainer & Bell Ltd., used by permission.*

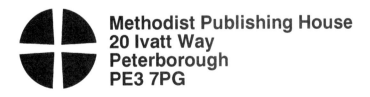